SOAP MAKING AND CANDLE MAKING BUSINESS

Lisa Graham

COPYRIGHT© 2020

All rights reserved. No part of this book may be reproduced or used in any form without the express written permission of the publisher except for the use of brief quotation in a book review.

First Printing 2020

ABOUT THE AUTHOR

I'm Lisa Graham, an expert in the production of soaps and candles. I cultivate this passion thanks to my grandmother, who passed on her art to me in the productions she made in her country house in Quebec, where I spent my childhood. For over 20 years, I have made this passion my main business; in fact, I collaborate both online and offline with the most important perfume distribution chain in Vancouver, which I can't name.

I don't deny that it took me years, in the making of soaps and candles, to develop the elements of the past properly and to modernize the methods I have learned over the years.

Still, I can say that I have finally found the best techniques that make my creations a real success, and I want to share all this with you, so that anyone can start a profitable business even from home, guiding you step by step towards the road to success!

TABLE OF CONTENT

INTRODUCTION	1
PART ONE: SOAP MAKING BUSINESS	2
CHAPTER 1	2
What Is Soap Making?	2
What About 21st Century Soaps?	3
How Soap Products Became Popular	3
How Soaps Get to Stores	3
Development of Modern Soaps	4
What Are Popular Soap Making Methods?	5
CHAPTER 2	6
Why Make Your Soap (objectives)	6
To Control What's in the Soap	7
To Create Beautiful, Useful Soap As Desire	7
Commercial Soap Making	8
Soap Making Safety Guidelines	10
Record Your Results and Learn from Your Errors	11
Wear Gloves	11
Research about your ingredients to have a better knowledge of them	12
Follow your Recipe Strictly	13
Take Care of Your Eyes	14
Fire Extinguisher	15
Taking Care of your skin	15
Ventilate your Room	16

Be Prepared for Spills _____ 16
Ensure you are using the right recipe _____ 16
Have all your soap ingredients and materials at hand _____ 16
Water, Not Vinegar _____ 16

CHAPTER 3 _____ 18

Soapmaking Equipment _____ 18

The equipment you will require includes: _____ 18
Sundry equipment or other equipment (slow cooker) _____ 23
Choosing Your Soap Making Ingredients _____ 24
What about pans that are enameled? _____ 25
Making Cold Process Soap _____ 25
Some Commonly Used Terms In Soap Making _____ 26
Natural Homemade Skin Care Product _____ 27
The step by step process. _____ 27

CHAPTER 4 _____ 35

Different Types of Soap _____ 35

Types of Soaps _____ 35
Types of Soaps Based on Usage _____ 35
1.   Toilet Soaps and Bathing Soaps _____ 35
2. Laundry Soaps _____ 36
3. Beauty Soaps/ Bars _____ 37
4. Novelty Soaps _____ 38
5. Guest Soaps _____ 38
6. Dish Soaps _____ 39
7. Medicated Soaps _____ 40
8. Non-Toilet Soaps _____ 41

9. Glycerin Soaps _____ 42
Types of Soaps Based on Form _____ 44
1. Handmade Soaps _____ 44
2. Bar Soaps _____ 45

CHAPTER 5 _____ 46

Handmade Soaps Which Bring Beauty and Style To Bathrooms 46

1. Homemade Detox Charcoal and Green Tea Soap _____ 46
2. Great Smelling Apple Tart Soap _____ 47
3. Easy DIY Avocado Oil Soap _____ 48
4. Adorable Homemade Bunny Soaps _____ 50
5. Colorful Sunflower Goat Milk Soap _____ 51
6. Homemade Chocolate Soap _____ 53
7. Coffee And Cream Soap _____ 54
8. Homemade Color Block Soap _____ 55
9. DIY Lavender Soap With Goat's Milk _____ 57
10. Adorable DIY Lollipop Soaps _____ 59
11. Homemade Pumpkin Vanilla Swirl Soap _____ 60
12. DIY Rose Petal Soaps _____ 62
13. Handmade Lemon And Rosemary Soap _____ 63
14. DIY Tie Dye Soap _____ 64
15. Cute Jewelry Box Soaps _____ 66

CHAPTER 6 _____ 69

All Natural Carrot Soap Recipe Using Real Carrots _____ 69

Natural Carrot Soap Recipe _____ 69
List of Soap-Making Methods _____ 75
1. Cold Process _____ 75

2. Hot Process _____ 76
3. Melt and Pour Soap _____ 76
4. Rebatching or Hand-Milled _____ 77
Explanation And Processing Of Hand Milled _____ 78
Three-Layered Soap _____ 78
Swirled Hand-Milled Soap Bars _____ 79
Melt-and-Pour Soap _____ 80
Primary Method for Making Melt-and-Pour Soap _____ 82
Layered Melt-and-Pour Designs _____ 83
Basic Layered Soaps with Piped-in Designs _____ 84
Embedding Botanicals _____ 85

CHAPTER 7 _____ 86

How Much Money Can I Make Online Selling Homemade Soap? 86

Product Appeal _____ 86
Way Of Selling _____ 87
How To Sell Soaps You Have Made? _____ 87
Selling Soap Legally & Regulations _____ 91
Selling Homemade Soap Online: Pros and Cons _____ 91
How You Can Market Your Handmade Soap Efficiently and Easily 92
Step 1: Prioritize Your Marketing Efforts _____ 93
Step 2: Strategize Your Marketing Efforts _____ 94
Step 3: Put Your Marketing Into Action _____ 98
Step 4: Repeat _____ 99
Let Us Go Further On How To Efficiently Market Your Soap products _____ 99
Decide which social networks you love most and will use _____ 100
Handle complaints in the right way and Give outstanding customer service _____ 102

Facebook Marketing techniques _____ 105
Facebook Marketing Basics _____ 107
Create Facebook Offers _____ 108
Paid Advertising Strategy on Facebook _____ 110
Twitter Tips: Make Your Tweets get to the Top _____ 112
Setup Strategy for Twitter Profile _____ 112
Paid Advertisement on Twitter _____ 115
Pinterest tips: the way to marketing excellence _____ 115
Advertising on Pinterest By Promoted Pins _____ 117
LinkedIn Tips: Network Like Clockwork _____ 117
YouTube Tips: Video Made the Marketing Star _____ 118
Paid Advertising on YouTube _____ 119
Instagram Tips: Snap-happy Marketing Strategy _____ 119

PART TWO: CANDLE MAKING BUSINESS _____ 121

CHAPTER 8 _____ 121

THE HISTORY AND LANGUAGE OF CANDLES _____ 121

The History of Candlemaking _____ 121
The Earliest Traces of Candlelight _____ 121
What is candle making business? _____ 124
The major expenses in a candle making business _____ 126
How much can you charge customers? _____ 131
How much profit can you earn in a candle-making business? _ 131
The best ways to increase the profitability of your Candle business?
_____ 132
The Nineteen Century Candle Making _____ 132
The Twenty-century candle making _____ 133
Nowadays Candles _____ 133

CHAPTER 9 — 135

MISTAKES TO AVOID WHEN BEGINNING A CANDLE-MAKING BUSINESS — 135

The Different Types Of Candles — 137
Container candles — 137
Ways of candle making — 139
Why you should Make Your Candles? — 140

CHAPTER 10 — 144

HOW TO GET STARTED IN CANDLE MAKING — 144

Equipment For Candle Making — 146
A Good Working Area — 163
Candle making Safety Or Precaution — 164
Candle Wax Additives — 169

CHAPTER 11 — 172

MOVING INTO CANDLE PRODUCTION — 172

The Candles And Recipes — 172
1. How to Make Soy candle — 172
2. How to Make Beautiful Ice candle — 176
3. How to Make another Ice Candles — 185
4. How to Make Shot Glass Candles — 187
5. Making Borax Candle Wicks — 191
6. Scented Tea Lights — 197
7. Melt the Wax — 199
8. Dipped Candles — 200
9. Natural Soy Wax Tea Lights — 201

10. Make a Gel Candle	206

CHAPTER 12 — 211

CANDLE MAKING AS A BUSINESS — 211

Candle Base Decorating Ideas	211
The Most Creative Candle Designs Ever	212
How to Make Hand Candles	212
Hand Gestures	215

CHAPTER 13 — 217

CANDLE MAKING AS A PROFITABLE BUSINESS — 217

Planning For Candle Making Success In Eight Steps	218
The Candle Business Marketing Guide	223
Getting New Candle Buyers With Internet advertising	226
Ensure Repeat Customers With Email Marketing	226
Marketing Concepts For Brick and Mortar Candle Businesses	227
Keep your Customers Interlocked With Your Candle Business	227
Unique Marketing Techniques To Start Your Candle Business	228
How much money can I make selling homemade candle online?	229
Types of candles that you can sell online	230
Type 1 – Scented or aromatherapy candles	230
Type 2 – Selling decorative candles	230
Type 3 – Soy and Vegan candles	231
Selling Homemade candle Online: Pros and Cons	231
Craft Shows, Festivals, Flea Markets	233
You need to tell your story	233

CHAPTER 14 — 235

CANDLE BUSINESS MARKETING ON SOCIAL MEDIA — 235

Candle Making Business Promotion On Social Media — 235
Facebook marketing — 240
Who Is To Employ Facebook For Candle Marketing — 241
How is a Facebook marketing campaign? — 242
Guide to using Facebook for business — 244
Twitter Marketing — 249
Instagram marketing — 251
Why Instagram Is Not Just for Aspiring Photographers — 251
LinkedIn Marketing — 252
1. Keep refining your LinkedIn profile — 253
2. Find highly targeted customers and connections — 254
3. Create an active LinkedIn page — 254
4. Define your audience and goals — 254
5. Post-high-quality content — 255
6. Add a LinkedIn "Follow" button or social media buttons to your website — 255
Youtube Marketing — 255
Use websites like Amazon, Etsy, and several others. — 261
How to market & promote your candle making business — 261
How to keep customers coming back — 262

CONCLUSION — 263

INTRODUCTION

If you enjoy what you do and are enthusiastic about it, anything else can clearly fit into position in your business.

Candle and soap making for profit is a great business idea for candles and soap loving people, and it is essential for them to understand the process of making candles and soap.

The real thing about candles and soap is that there is an un-endless supply of scents you can make to attract anyone.

Immediately you discover ways to make the long-lasting soap and long-smelling candles; you can probably find a steadfast stream of buyers.

People love candles, even if it is just for decoration in their houses.

However, this candle-making and soap-making business don't really cost anything to begin, so it's extremely profitable as long as you understand how to sell your candle and soap making business.

This could also become a perfect opportunity for moms to remain at home and easily begin their own business so that they can be home with their kids and have a flexible job.

You will discover and understand everything you need to create candles and soap at home in this book and transform it into a profitable business.

PART ONE: SOAP MAKING BUSINESS

CHAPTER 1

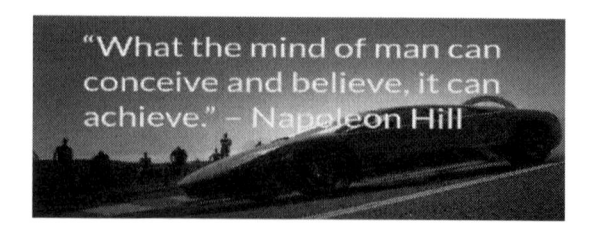

> "What the mind of man can conceive and believe, it can achieve." – Napoleon Hill

What Is Soap Making?

World War 1 contributed to the usage of synthetic detergents, and the scarcity of easily available animal fat demanded a particular supply of fatty acids for homemade soap. To this purpose, we use vegetable oils today. Moreover, the ashes used throughout history were modified, and the active ingredient extracted and today we use sodium hydroxide.

For hundreds of years, people have produced soap to help clean dirt and oil from their bodies, dishes, surfaces, floor, or clothes. Individuals have needed to produce soap at home in the past, as it was not available in stores. At home, soap making was a time-consuming, messy, and hot procedure that many people performed only once a year.

What About 21st Century Soaps?

Currently, the industrial soap that you and your family are using follows a standard formula, and is also being manufactured in a pretty close manner as it was about a hundred years earlier, shortly after the industrial revolution. However, the ways the producers have changed involve rendering soap milder on the skin, soap coloring, and its scent.

How Soap Products Became Popular

Entrepreneurs in many geographical regions have established factories to produce specialized soaps with a transparent type with a distinctive and delicate fragrance.

Since people also needed laundry soap, manufacturers started grinding soap with a mortar and pestle to make flakes that rapidly dissolved in warm water. By the late 18th century, soap making became a huge business with the opening of large industries in major cities. Many of those industries still operate today, producing various soaps and laundry types. Intensive advertisement for soap in newspapers and magazines caused individuals to buy soaps in retail shops quickly.

How Soaps Get to Stores

Many modern soaps are manufactured with either hot or cold chemical processes in large quantities in huge industries. Hot soap methods differ in temperatures such as boiling, dry, or standard formats; cold soap manufacturing is the most common way of making hard soaps utilizing the old-fashioned combining of lye and water.

When the soap has been prepared, it is put to dry in molds in various shapes and sizes. For strong soaps, the average drying time is three days. The products are packaged in cloth, acrylic, or cardboard containers when the soaps are fully dry and hardened. Large quantities of packed soaps are delivered by buses or trains into stores and malls, people who shop for soap nowadays hope to find a corridor lined with product choices.

Development of Modern Soaps

Every soap manufacturer uses special formulas that contain unique ingredients. This expertise renders it a distinctive product, which different customers crave. Companies also produced formulations that use pumice grains to produce a solid soap that extracts thick dirt like grease. Optionally, soft soaps are made for the baby's fragile skin. There are soap formulae for deodorizing or medicating the skin. Medicated soaps can help to prevent acne or to ease itchy dermatitis. Antibacterial soaps have lately become common to deter infections from spreading. Both strong and liquid antibacterial soaps are widely used for the removal of bacteria in bathrooms and kitchens.

What Are Popular Soap Making Methods?

If you're puzzled about the whole method of producing the soap, you're about to find out. You probably heard people speaking about the cold method, the hot method, melting and pouring, rebatching, and maybe discussing the package for soap making. Soap manufacturing relates to the direct production of fresh soap to professional soap-makers. That is to say, you start with soap making materials, lye, and oils, mixing them and producing soap that doesn't exist before.

CHAPTER 2

Why Make Your Soap (objectives)

Many people do not want to make soap from scratch. They love soap decoration instead of making soap. Because of the first stage of mixing products to make an effective soap, they want to concentrate on the design, colors, scents, and swirls. When some people speak of making soap, they often think of "melting and pouring" and "rebatching." Soap is not made from scratch using these techniques. You take and melt soap that was already produced. You smooth it over instead and proceed to decorate it.

Making your soap is exciting, and it helps you to make every size, color, form, and scent of soaps. When you're producing the soap, you know what's going into it. You can add any ingredients you need, such as spices, herbal fragrances, moisturizers, etc. Below are prominent soap making procedures, and each of these methods uses a few different ingredients to create a soap that turns out to be right.

Envisage using your homemade beautiful soap bar. If you've used soap that you've made utilizing modern methods, there's no turning back to the store where it is bought. There's a tremendous satisfaction to say, "oh, I've made this." So maybe that's the primary reason why you made the soap.

To Control What's in the Soap

In addition to the hands-on aspect of using homemade soap, there are also other reasons for making it yourself. One of the most important things is that you can control exactly what you are using to make your soap, and therefore determine what you and your family are using to take a bath. For instance, several soap-makers began out of a desire to reduce an allergic reaction of a child to commercial soap.

Most people who've never been willing to comfortably use other consumer soaps discover that they can use homemade soap. They might be more prone to industrial soap non-soap components, instead of the soap itself. Invigorate friends and relatives who are sensitive enough to seek homemade soaps.

To Create Beautiful, Useful Soap As Desire

Another reason many people make soap is a desire to produce something beautiful and useful. Motivation may vary from trying to catch a favorite flower's essence to finding an excellent complement for a newly painted bathroom color. All decorative components that can be mixed into a single bar of soap are the elegance of herbs and flowers, the unity of well-orchestrated light, and the sensory pleasure of varying textures.

Of course, as well as being beautiful, handmade soap is also useful. What could be nicer than a soap bar? It does one simple, important aspect, no matter how stylish and glamorous you make it.

Soap doesn't just clean skin; you can create a soap to clean hair, clothing, dishes, dogs, carpets, etc. It is possible to wash almost everything that can be washed with handmade soap.

Commercial Soap Making

Commercially available soap is most frequently manufactured on a wide scale using the most cost-effective means possible. This involves the usage of chemical detergents, hardening compounds, and other very harmful chemicals on the skin. Even the additives of industrial soap render your hands dry as they focus on washing and fail to pamper your face. When producing handmade soap, it's produced with good materials including Lye and good oils. You could also control, for instance, what you add in it, by putting natural aromatherapy oils or substances like glycerin. Glycerin is a tiny amino acid, very beneficial for skin softness. The method of producing soap generates glycerin naturally. Many industrial soaps do, though, contain little glycerin. That is because they extract it for other skin-loving and high-quality items such as moisturizing lotions. This renders the soap rough and unpleasant to the skin though it cleans well. But on the skin, soap needs to be skin-friendly and soft too. You can incorporate glycerin or whatever skin-friendly product you choose to use, with natural homemade soap. You might claim that Lye is used in handmade soap, so you don't want Lye on your hands.

The marvel of chemistry is that in the saponification procedure, the Lye dissolves and mixes entirely with the oils used to make soap, so if you have used the right amounts, there is no more lye remaining. One of the most significant benefits of producing your soap is you can be assured about all the ingredients in it. You have 100% over it. You may opt to use all-natural goods, both herbal to skin-friendly methods and coloring can be used.

Another beauty to make your soap is being the control of the process. How you like your soap to smell is in your control. Need to keep it smooth or hard? Which fragrance do you like to use on your soap? Want to make the soap frothy and lathery, or just a little lather? All of this can be controlled by modifying the lye proportions and the type of oils you are using. Using castor oil, for example, offers you better outcomes than using olive oil, and so on. The possibilities for handmade soap are virtually infinite.

Soapmaking may be an experience that transforms life. DIY soap is an enjoyable and soothing activity to use to alleviate stress. Therefore, de-stressing is a perfect outlet for doing something different. Experimenting with various proportions and materials is a perfect way to convey and explore your creativity. Moreover, the designs of the molds, color variations, petal additions, as well as the final packaging, may also be innovative. This will also be great as an activity involving the bonding of arts and crafts. Your homemade soap should make you feel proud of your success and development, as you can see your bathroom shelves lined with your hands 'amazing work.

Soap making can also be your opportunity to boost your income because you can produce and sell homemade soap using your artistic touch and create your brand. Homemade soap has helped many females take care of their families by the selling of the soap they produce. Moreover, offering your friends, relatives or loved ones is an imaginative, and a lovely sensual present. There are lots of reasons to create your soap, let's dig into how you should create your soap without any hesitation. And, as ever, safety comes first, so let us discuss these safety precautions when making soap at home.

Soap Making Safety Guidelines

Work with a Clear Space

In any method, Clutter always is an enormous obstruction. The odds of error improve with a lot of debris. Ensure that you have a clear working space.

Record Your Results and Learn from Your Errors

It's essential to record the batch results so you can find out what went bad and prevent it in the future.

- Keep Pets and Children Away
- Label the Utensils you used for Lye
- Be cautious but don't let that inhibit your creativity from decreasing your fun

Wear Gloves

Standard rubber kitchen gloves offer sufficient protection for the lower arms and hands. Ensure there is a textured finger-hold on the gloves you purchase so that you can maintain a tight hold on your equipment. Some soap makers choose heavy-duty gloves. Only make sure that you have free use of your fingertips.

Thin "test" gloves can handle the partially cured soap. They can be sold in a large scale-market store's pharmacy section and drugstores. If you're latex allergic, you should purchase thin vinyl or neoprene gloves. Check the holes and breaks on your gloves frequently. Replace them until the need occurs.

When the soapmaking job is done for the day, clean the gloves well using soap and water. When you clean them and dry them, they are going to last for a time. Pull them inside out to dry, then store them after it has dried.

Make sure to cover your body with a long-sleeved top over the gloves. The large button-up shirt with roll-up sleeves is perfect.

These health measures are not intended to frighten you; but, keeping protection first, enjoyment second, is still of prime importance. When you're confident all the protection precautions are in effect, you can relax and enjoy the soapmaking fun!

Clearly understand that you won't be carelessly splashing Lye about. You'll have it prepared, and you won't be running around, dripping caustics and hot soap. Only use common sense to make confident that you are covering yourself to household surfaces. Working with Lye and triggering a chemical reaction requires vigilance when these procedures are attempted.

Research about your ingredients to have a better knowledge of them

You should take your time to identify the ingredients before beginning. Lye is a material to be carefully handled.

For example, if you spill lye water, don't try to neutralize it with vinegar. You have to clean it with excess water, rather. If it has splashed onto the eyes or mouth or face, rinsing it with water is the only and safest way to prevent face or eye damage. When it runs out on the clothing, quickly wash the contaminated items.

Follow your Recipe Strictly

Chemical reactions will occur in a form. It all leads to proportions. Too much, or lesser of anything, may have an unintended impact. In soap production, all the ingredients in the formula are specified by weight, sometimes ounces as residues of each ingredient are used.

So, it would be perfect if you had your recipe written out so that rather than fumbling with your phone or tablet when dealing with your materials, particularly Lye, you might avoid pouring everything out. It could take you to memorize the recipe by heart a couple of days, and then it will be much simpler.

The next thing you need to be specifically following the recipes is a sensitive scale. Use a kitchen scale of decent quality or a digital scale. Be sure that you first try it out with certainly proven weights, including a measured weight coin, to check the accuracy of the balance. When checked, you will measure all the ingredients according to your recipe. It is not advisable to alter something at the start.

Few recipes mention quantities rather than weights and may be used to adjust recipes according to the preferred volume, although it is wise to start with a pre-written recipe at the beginning.

Take Care of Your Eyes

Your eyes should be among your top health goals. A lot of stuff can go wrong and get into your eye during soap making, but by wearing protection lab goggles, you can address the problem.

Lye or raw soap or dye powder could get into your eyes through any means, but not if you have protection goggles on. You would never miss the move anyway. You do need access to water nearby to wash it just in case. Get anti-fog goggles, if you want optimum visibility.

Ensure sure eye safety is damage safe, caustic, and heat immune. If you are using glasses, use goggles large enough to fit over them. Be precise when searching for eye protection.

Never take risks with your eyes for health and protection. The danger to your eyes is attributable to the risk of lye particles, lye water, fresh soap, hot oils, and other substances that splash you in the face.

The main dangers of methods that do not use caustics to produce soap are hot molten soap and steam. You'll experience very little if any splashing incidents as long as you're operating attentively. Most soap makers use a full-face mask, which can be flipped up or down when they are operating.

In the very least, caustics on the face can induce surface damage to the skin. At worst, if you splash lye solution into your eyes, you can become blind. Make sure to have an emergency strategy just in case anything bad occurs.

Fire Extinguisher

Any time you work with a burner, hotplate, or other types of fuel, you should have a fire extinguisher within reach.

Make sure your fire extinguisher is loaded and ready use. The moment you use the extinguisher for the fire is not the time to ask where it is, or if it is loaded. Review the instructions, and you know how to use it. Also, be sure to review core safety procedures in the kitchen. For instance, you can never pour water on an oil fire, and while holding hot pans and utensils, you should still wear protective mitts.

Taking Care of your skin

The same is true for your face, just like your eyes. Unless you weren't wearing safety gloves, Lye or raw soap could be incredibly painful to the skin. Latex gloves should be used. Dishwashing gloves are also fine to work in, but they can be cumbersome to work with. You may even cover the skin by adding an apron or long-sleeved shirt so you won't be exposed.

Ventilate your Room

Working with a chemical reaction and the raw soap residue in locked windows is not advisable. Hold the windows open to breathe fresh air in the space that you are in.

Be Prepared for Spills

Even when you're wearing safety clothing, it might happen. Hence, getting a plan B is often necessary. So, keep this nearby and have a granular absorbent or universal absorbent spill pack. The leak may be tar, soap, Lye, and so on. Always have a supply of water near.

Ensure you are using the right recipe

Sometimes, lots of people can write anything on the Internet without having the proper information of the percentages and calculations. Make sure you get recipes from trusted sources. You can use the recipes in this book.

Have all your soap ingredients and materials at hand

When you start, there will not be time to go around gathering all your ingredients. Keep everything set and within hands range before you begin.

Water, Not Vinegar

Traditionally, vinegar was used as a neutralizer for lye leaks and untreated soap leaks. You shouldn't dump vinegar into an alkaline skin spill, though. That would be a good idea to let your doctor know you're making soap, and ask about how best to deal with caustic skin contact. When you come into contact with a lye or raw soap paste, carefully clean the drop off your skin.

Then flush with dirt, then wash with water and soap. Do not hesitate to finish mixing the mixture until a layer of fresh soap is stripped and rinsed off your hands. Use it as soon as it touches you.

CHAPTER 3

Soapmaking Equipment

Soap manufacturing requires specific cooking appliances, so although you may want to use your regular saucepans. Hence, utensils, I highly encourage you to buy a package that you hold strictly for manufacturing soaps.

You may produce soap in a stainless-steel saucepan on any form of hob - electric, gas, induction.

The equipment you will require includes:

Saucepan

If you're going to produce soap on the hob, you'll need a heat-proof pan, like that of a saucepan. The pan must be made of stainless steel to prevent any unpleasant reaction with the lye.

Spatula

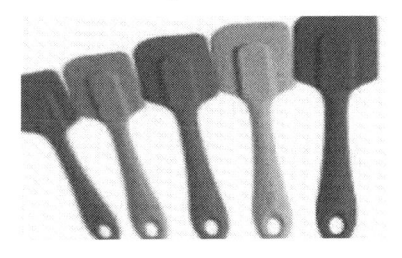

You can use a long-handled spatula to scrap the traces of soap off the surfaces of the pan and jugs.

Silicone spatulas are highly flexible and, therefore, can endure soap mixture heat.

Spoons

A selection of dessert spoons, stainless steel teaspoons, and serving spoons to stir and dispense ingredients will be needed.

Jugs and bowls

You'll need to have a heat-proof container or cup to mix in the lye solution. While these can be made of thick plastic, they will deteriorate after using it for months, so the heatproof glass is preferable.

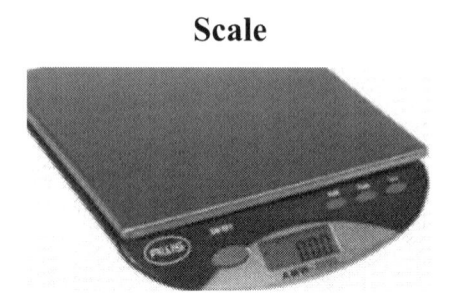

Scale

The best method to measure soap-making materials is by weight, so you need the correct scale. It is not accurate or precise to measure by volume.

If you are dealing in small quantities, inaccuracies in measuring are intensified. An ounce of oil, more or less, in a quantity which has a total weight of 12 pounds, does not make a significant difference. Yet one ounce short or extra in a 1-pound mixture is a big difference and will render a product either too alkaline or too oily.

The economy shouldn't be the prime concern when looking for scales. You need accuracy, simplicity of use, and the potential to manage the quantity of materials in the product size you produce. Search for a tare-function scale, which implies it resets to zero as ingredients are put on it. Watch out for measurements weighing grams and ounces.

You could scrimp on several of your materials for soapmaking but place the money on a decent scale. With trust, comfort, and peace of mind, it will repay you over and over. You can purchase an exquisite scale with little money, and you can use it for years. Protecting the wireless scale under plastic wrap or in a plastic bag with zip closure is a great idea so that the keypad is not damaged.

A handheld stick blender

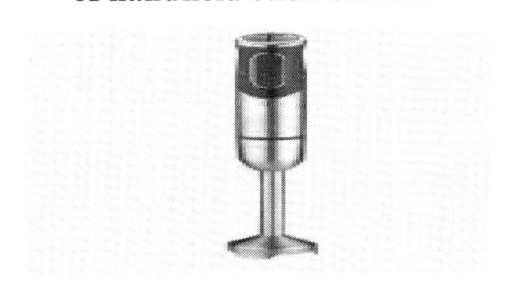

This is such handy equipment. Any soap maker must have this in their toolbox! While the soap can be produced without a handheld stick blender, if you have one, it can save hours of stirring. Molds (with or without a mold liner and something to hold the liner in place) Until your soap is finished, it must be poured into your selected molds.

Many molds can need lining to allow the finished soap easy to extract, in which case you might need pegs or tape to keep the liner in place.

Old towels and blankets

If you use the cold-process process, you may need to insulate your soap within the first 24 hours. To do so efficiently, cover the soap with layers of towels or cloths.

Protective clothing

And if you don't need total overalls, at least you'll require safety goggles, safety gloves, and an apron. They protect the hands, eyes, and clothes from any accidental caustic splashes.

Kitchen towels, paper, cloths, and hot water

Soap making can be very messy! Have a roll of kitchen paper towels or cloths at hand to clear up any spillages.

Sundry equipment or other equipment (slow cooker)

Slow Cooker

In this book, all the hot-process recipes call for the use of a slow cooker. You will need a three-quarter slow cooker with high and low heat settings and detachable crock section. Don't use a slow food cooker again that has used for making soap.

In hot-process recipes, the slow cooker must be just the right size for the batch that you produce. If it becomes too small or too large, it is not going to process the soap properly. This can overheat, gush, or scorch. Examine the recipe for the size requirements.

Stock Pot

In this book, ideal for the cold-process 4-and 8-pound recipes is stainless- steel stockpots. An 8-quarter will contain 4-pound recipes, and 8-pound recipes will be kept in a 12-quarter stock bowl, with space to mix. It's helpful, but it is not required if the stock pots have gradation marks indicating the volume.

Pots and Pans

The stainless steel is the best choice when you are purchasing your soapmaking pots and pans. In a restaurant supply, supermarket, sale, and thrift shops, you can purchase stainless steel pots and pans at incredibly fair prices.

What of In-oxidable Steel? And you don't have to use nonstick, copper, cast iron, or tin they're going to react with the soaps, destroying soap and brush. Seek not just "just to see." They'll react badly perhaps violently and toxically with the lye used in the process of soap making.

Choosing Your Soap Making Ingredients

You may produce soap powder, sodium hydroxide, and fat using a few like three ingredients. Even if you have an option of fats, if you want to make 'true' soap, there is no alternative for sodium hydroxide, as this induces the chemical reaction, which ultimately transforms the fats into soap.

Sodium And Potassium Hydroxide

Authentic, natural soap, both hard bar and liquid soap, are made from the chemical reaction of lye combined with fats. The lye is made from water (or water mixed with other liquids) and an alkali. For bars of soap, the sodium hydroxide is alkali; for liquid soaps, the potassium hydroxide is alkali.

What about pans that are enameled?

Many soap makers use enameled pots without encountering any problem of any kind at all, but you have to check it for holes and nicks that will expose the soap to the reactive metal beneath. For example, I saw a soapmaking recipe years ago, and it seemed interesting to me. So, I brought in all the ingredients together. And the instructions stated that they were cautious about lye fumes, but they did not mention not to use an aluminum container. My pan happened to be an aluminum, so black smoke began coming out of the pan after applying the lye solution. I thought that the lye smokes were the reason why it was so. Few minutes later, I had a black soap ball trapped in it with a spatula, and a ruined pot! I realized this could not be right.

Making Cold Process Soap

Cold process soap is produced by mixing oils and sodium hydroxide lye.

The cold method is a perfect choice if you want to customize the soap down to the last ingredient. You can choose oils, dyes, scents, and more. If you've discovered the right recipe, the designs will get you creative. Cold process soap is made with a mixture of oils and sodium hydroxide lye, which induces saponification, a chemical reaction. Soap has already been through the process of melting and pouring.

Some Commonly Used Terms In Soap Making

Trace: That is the stage that it emulsifies the oils and the lye water. A tiny trace, there should be no traces of oil, and the soap will be the thin cake batter's consistency. As the soap settles and begins to form, it will begin to thicken to a moderate and thick trace.

Gel phase: Soap becomes as hot as 180 ° F during the gel process, and produces a gelatinous look. Gelled soap has a lighter hue, with a somewhat shiny appearance, and it can be unmolded faster too. Some manufacturers force their soap with covers and heating pads through a gel-phase. The gel process isn't mandatory, though – it's a personal choice. This influences the bar look and not the quality. Ungelled soap has a matte look. Placing the soap in a cooler for a day will prevent the gel process.

Curing: basically, it is possible to use cold process soap after a couple of days. We recommend letting the soap cure in a calm, dry spot with good airflow for 4-6 weeks, though. Excess water can evaporate, making harder and milder bars in the shower to last longer.

Lye Calculator: This tool makes recipes of cold processes simple to formulate. What you need to do is input the weight or percentage of the oil and the Lye Calculator will give you the quantity of lye and liquid you need for your recipe. It calculates the level of super fat.

Soda ash: This produces an irregular, dry, whitish soap because When un-saponified lye reacts with naturally occurring carbon dioxide in the soil, it forms. The consistency is not affected, so the soap is safe to use. It may also hide more complex designs or render the bars feel crumbly. With several tricks, like a 10 percent water discount and gel process, you can prevent it.

Natural Homemade Skin Care Product

RECIPES
- 26.5 ounces of Olive oil
- 16.5 ounces of Coconut oil
- 10 ounces of Palm oil
- 209 grams of Lye
- 2.7 ounces - the optional scent of Your choice of essential oils
- 20 ounces of Distilled water

The step by step process.

Step 1: Measure out the 209 grams of dry lye. You can do this by filling a resealable bag with the sodium hydroxide and weigh it on a digital scale.

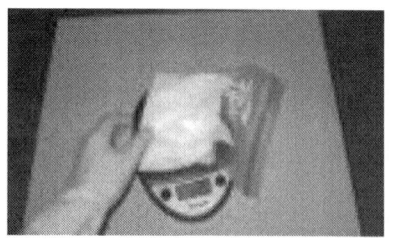

Step 2: In a heat-safe jar measure out the 20 ounces of distilled water.

Step 3: Pour the lye cautiously into the water from the re-sealable bottle, while briskly stirring the solution with a plastic, heavy-duty rubber or wooden utensil. Continue to mix until the lye is dissolved. The reaction produced by mixing lye and water will heat this mixture, so be cautious!

Step 4: Put a thermometer in the solution for lye/water and safely put aside for later use. For it to be used, the temperature must be lowered to around 95 degrees Fahrenheit.

Step 5: Measure 26.5 ounces of olive oil, 16.5 ounces of coconut oil, and 10 ounces of palm oil. It could be best for the beginner to do so in different glass containers.

Step 6: use a 3-quart saucepan to melt the two solid oils (the coconut oil and palm oil) to liquid form. You should use low heat if you don't wish to burn the oil.

Step 7: add liquefied coconut oil, olive oil, and liquefied palm oil to the big soap making pot and put your soap in it using a thermometer for the solution.

Step 8: next, wait patiently for the soap making oils and lye/water solution to cool.

Before continuing, mixtures must have the same temperature of 95 degrees Fahrenheit. In most situations, to make them correct, you'll need to change the temperatures significantly, because it's uncommon for all mixtures to reach the same temperature at the same time themselves.

When any combination dropped below 95 degrees, the temperature may be increased by putting the whole pot in a sink and filling it with hot water. Alternately you should place the pot in a sink filled with cold water when you need to cool a mixture that its temperature is too high. Do so before the temperatures are appropriate!

Step 9: You're able to produce soap now that the temperatures are accurate! In the big soap pot, gradually apply the lye/water solution to the oil mixture.

Constantly stir in a figure-eight design to ensure that the lye and oils connect during this process. You should use a stick blender for a faster trace.

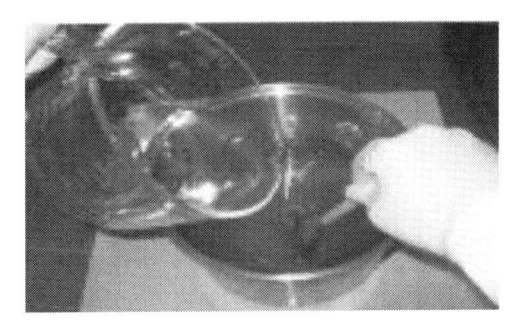

Step 10: Watch out for trace. Check for this by drizzling a tiny volume of the mixture across the mixture surface from your mixing utensil. If the liquid stays for a short time on top of the surface before sinking into the mixture again, then note that trace has occurred. You will realize that there's been saponification because when that occurs, that means that the soap is ready.

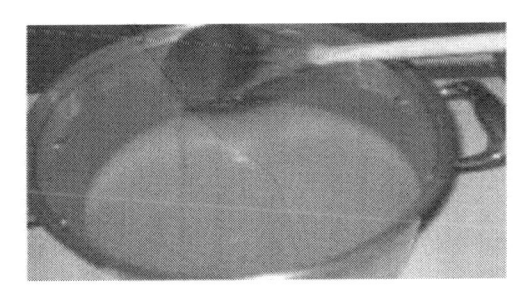

Please note that you can need to stir up to an hour, or as little as eight minutes. While this is a simple soap recipe, the most challenging part of any cold process soap making project, particularly for the beginner, is noticing trace before it's too late. I suggest you check for trace every 5-10 minutes to make sure you're not missing anything.

If you stir your soap after the trace has happened, the soap will begin to solidify in your bowl, so you will not be able to pour it into the mold that forms the soap. Note that the trace should appear even faster if you are using a driven stick blender.

Therefore, modify judiciously!

Step 13: pour the soap into the mold very fast. This is a 5-pound recipe of soap making, and you can use a 5-pound mold. If an extra solution sticks to the surface of the soap-making tub, leave it! There's a reasonable chance this additional residue hasn't been used in the saponification reaction.

Step 14: now is the time to get the soap insulated. To protect it from the air, put a cover, a sheet of cardboard, or heavy-duty freezer paper on top of the mold. To insulate the mold further, cover it in a few blankets or many towels.

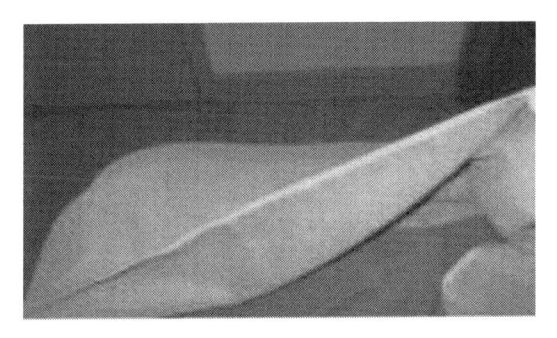

Step 15: Let the soap sit uninterrupted/unchecked for about 24 - 36 hours.

Step 16: When the new product is solid enough to cut, extract it from the mold and cut the loaf into bars using a soap cutter (must be within 24-36 hours based on the recipe). If you have a wooden soap mold with a built-in cutting hole, you can use it to cut flat bars and make it straight.

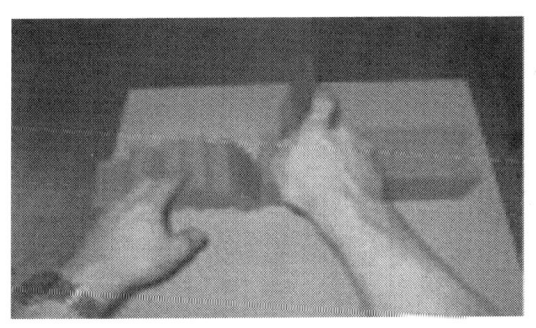

Step 17: Position each bar on a cookie rack to further solidify. Flip them over once a week, intervals. Your soap will be excellent and ready for use after 4-6 weeks.

Be careful to remove the white powder, which might have formed on the soap surface before using it or selling it.

The white ash is referred to as soda ash.

Step 18: Constantly check the soap's PH levels before using it if you are a beginner.

CHAPTER 4

Different Types of Soap

Types of Soaps

Will you want to wash your face with the exact soap you use to wash your clothes? No. Why do you think so? It's so because you realize that it is based on what has to be washed that determines the type of soap that is used. But have you ever asked if there are other forms of soaps, and what makes them different?

There are several forms of soaps that are focused on the process used to produce them and the reason for which they are used.

Types of Soaps Based on Usage

- Toilet Soaps
- Non-Toilet Soaps
- Glycerin Soaps
- Transparent Soaps

1. Toilet Soaps and Bathing Soaps

Toilet soaps and bathing soaps are those for cosmetic use. The words toilet soap and bathing soap are used interchangeably. They're not the same thing, though, and have major variations between them.

Since all of these are used in hygiene, their composition differs.

On the other side, bathing soaps do have lower TFM. In terms of cleaning, that renders them superior to toilet soaps. Bathing bars should be considered as soaps at the entry point because their TFM benefit is comparatively high compared to toilet soaps.

Toilet soaps are grouped into three grades based on their TFM value, and afterward, their cleaning ability.

2. Laundry Soaps

Laundry soaps are distributed in the form of liquid, powder, and gel. Soaps were produced with all-natural materials back then though which includes goat fat and wood ash. But as demand grew and natural resources became limited, the use of synthetic materials became widespread. Hence what you have at your fingertips today are detergents and not soaps.

Detergents include surface-active chemicals, or surfactants, found in all soaps in the laundry. The surfactant properties differ from brand to brand.

Surfactants are liable for extracting dirt from the laundry. These surfactant molecules have two ends; one end is drawn to water (hydrophilic end), and the other end is drawn to dirt (hydrophobic end). The hydrophobic part of a surfactant molecule is bound to the dirt, and the dirt is washed away from the surface with a rinse of water.

3. Beauty Soaps/ Bars

As the name suggests, beauty bars are cleaning products that are intended to be used on the skin. They are suitable for various skin shapes and skin disorders, and you might want to pick a beauty bar that fits your skin tone. Beauty bars are essential for the reduction of acne and dark spot, improvement of fairness, etc., and they often help to provide a moisturizing and hydrating impact on the skin.

As already stated, soap is a substance produced from natural ingredients. However, some of the cleaning items commonly available are detergents.

Therefore, several brands name their beauty detergents "beauty bars" rather than "beauty soaps." Beauty soaps in the shape of tubes, liquid washes and gels are available. They come in numerous colors, have varying proportions, and often are scented. One popular feature of all beauty bars is that they cleanse the face and kill bacteria.

4.Novelty Soaps

Novelty soaps serve as being more than just a cleaning agent. They are physically pleasing and act as a source of fun for children in particular. They come in several colors, forms, and patterns, such as a duck, cat, vehicle, etc. They may be seen as bathroom decoration or as a source of inspiration for children who don't like taking baths.

They have a pleasant scent and are made mainly by hand. They are sometimes offered as presents because of the range of colors, forms, and sizes.

5. Guest Soaps

Guest soaps are just the visitor's soaps. Similar to the regular soaps, they are physically more appealing, and little in size. These are the soaps that you can find in your hotel rooms. Many people like to have guest soaps in their bathrooms while they have frequent visitors. There is no particular intention behind such soaps other than to give an outstanding impression to the visitors. Guest soaps are usually oval, shell-shaped, or floral.

6. Dish Soaps

Dish soap, dish detergent, or dishwasher liquid is a special form of soap meant for washing up dishes. Many dish soaps produce powerful chemicals, which means they cannot be used on the skin. What distinguishes dish soaps from normal, skin-friendly soaps is the large number of surfactants that dish soaps contain. That's why dishwashing soaps will not only disinfect the oils on the dishes but also strip off the oil and grease.

Dish soaps contain plenty of foam. Many come as a concentrate and must be dissolved in water, whereas others come in condensed ways. Many dish soaps contain ingredients such as lemon and mint that leave behind a soothing fragrance after the plates are cleaned.

7.Medicated Soaps

Medicated soaps are specialized soaps containing ingredients formulated to treat one or more skin issues. Acne, blackheads, pimples, rashes, clogged pores, and fungal and bacterial infections are among the skin infections which can be handled with medicated soaps. Medicated soaps formulations vary based on the disease a specific soap is intended to treat.

There are numerous forms of medicated soaps that are effective in treating skin problems. They are listed below:

Antibacterial Soaps

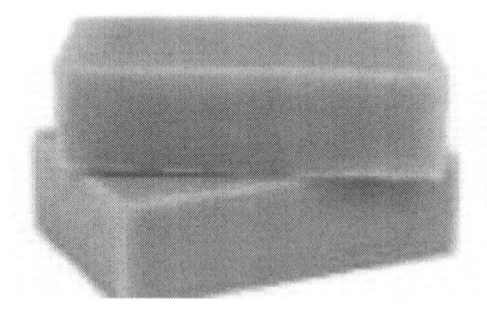

So-called antibacterial soaps, they include antibacterial agents such as triclosan, triclocarban, PCMX, tetrasodium EDTA, etc. Such soaps are intended to be added to skin infected by bacterial infections.

Antifungal Soaps

Antifungal soaps include antimicrobial agents to combat fungal skin infections. Which include organic medicinal plant extracts, essential oils, vitamin E, sulfur, natural glycerin, tea tree oil, zinc oxide, etc.

Medicated Soaps for Skin Problems

The skin is susceptible to many skin conditions, including bacterial and fungal infections such as clogged pores, fat cellulite, or even dry skin. One of the common skin disorders is Acne, and different medicated soaps are designed to treat acne. Such soaps include Neem and other plant extracts that can smooth the skin.

8. Non-Toilet Soaps

Non-toilet soaps are soaps used to purify toxic water. These soaps are used for eliminating rough oils. Most generally, they are called lithium soaps. They are the lithium salt of a fatty acid.

Although toilet soaps are used in home washing, lithium soaps are lithium grease components. Mixing lithium soap and oil is formed into lithium grease and is used as a thickener and lubricating agent.

9. Glycerin Soaps

Glycerin soaps are perhaps the most moisturizing soap types. They are sensitive to the skin. This kind of soap does not only moisturize the skin but is amazingly good for all kinds of skin. Glycerin soaps can make the skin appear healthy and moisturized.

Those soaps are 100% natural, rendering them ideal for delicate skin. People with delicate skin sometimes claim that bar soaps make their skin appear rough or make their skin conditions worse. These skin problems were attributed to synthetic chemicals being used in daily beauty bar soap. Glycerin soaps are therefore ideal also for the most susceptible bodies. If you do have extreme skin conditions such as psoriasis or eczema, glycerin soaps can work well for you.

Glycerin is a moisturizer, which means it attracts moisture. As a potential outcome, the skin is not only moisturized by using glycerin soap, but even the moisture is kept in. For many hours the skin should remain hydrated, making it appear new and smooth. If you consistently use glycerin wash, the skin will become smooth, and also it will feel suppler.

4. Transparent Soaps

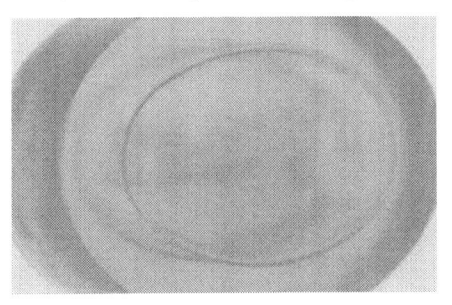

Like irregular soaps, transparent and see-through soaps are simple.
This is mixed in a hot alcohol solution, instead of adding and mixing soap content in water. Particles which remain undissolved in alcohol are filtered out, creating a clear soap.

The filtration of undissolved particles must be performed with great caution when processing transparent soaps, as such particles cannot be contained in an opaque mass, unlike normal bar soaps. In the distillation phase, the alcohol content is then removed from the mixture, so the residual left behind can form a solid mass. Transparent soaps are very strong, so they are very challenging to lather with.

Transparent soaps are not as moisturizing as vague soap bars; however, for skin dryness and acne, they are preferably efficient. This is how the alcohol during the process neutralizes the soap, and they are very versatile and can be wheezed into several forms or shapes.

Types of Soaps Based on Form

Soaps aren't just classified based on their usage; they can also be categorized on the basis of their form. Below, we look at the different types of soap based on their form. Soaps are not only graded due to their usage; they may also be listed according to their type. Below, we look at the various soap types, based on their form.

1. Handmade Soaps

Handmade soaps are more costly than commonly manufactured soaps. They're made from all-natural materials in limited quantities. Handmade soaps are authentic soaps since they contain only natural ingredients.

They're made of base oils such as palm oil, olive oil, coconut oil, and shea butter. These ingredients are abundant in the antioxidants, nutrients, and vitamins necessary for the protection of the skin.

Not only are homemade soaps soft on the hands, but they're healthier too. Since they do not contain any solid, toxic chemicals, humans with sensitive skin may use them.

2. Bar Soaps

"Bar soap" is a paragliding word that encompasses all types of soaps found in the form of a bar shape. That includes skin beauty soaps, soaps for baths, and soaps for washing or laundry soaps.

CHAPTER 5

Handmade Soaps Which Bring Beauty and Style To Bathrooms

1. Homemade Detox Charcoal and Green Tea Soap

These small charcoal soaps have a dark color, which would be perfect to introduce to your bathroom a matching color. To make them look lovely, you can shape them in soap or candy molds, and they have activated green and charcoal tea, two ingredients that are suitable to help clear up damaged skin. If you don't like green tea oil scent, you can add peppermint oil, and have the same results.

This active charcoal soap formula, detoxifying (and oh-so-easy), is perfect for skin that is prone to acne!

Equipment
- Double broiler
- Soap mold

RECIPES
- 1/2-pound shea butter soap base
- Five activated charcoal capsules if you can't find at a pharmacy you can buy online or one teaspoon of powder
- 15-20 drops tea tree essential oil

INSTRUCTIONS

Cut the base of the soap into tiny chunks, then heat over a double boiler.

Drop a small amount of soap into a cup, cool slightly, then add in charcoal, then add to the remainder of the soap base melted.

Add the tea tree oil. If you do not like tea tree fragrance, you may apply basic peppermint oil to conceal the scent.

Pour in the mold and let it cool (you can use a muffin tin).

2. Great Smelling Apple Tart Soap

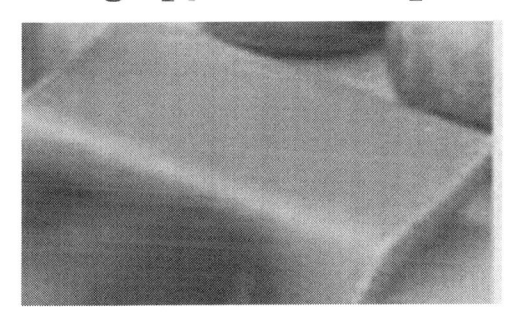

These are great for holidays with apple pie scent and cinnamon, or you might use them if you wish to give your bathroom a stunning, homey smell. You can shape them into tiny little tart cups to make them appear like little apple tarts and also paint them red and green if you want to change its color a little bit.

RECIPES
- 4oz. (115g) Clear Glycerin Soap base
- 1/2 Tsp Ground Cinnamon
- 3 Drops Red Food Color
- 1 Tbs Liquid Soap
- 1 Tsp Liquid Glycerin
- 1/2 tsp Apple Pie Fragrance Oil

INSTRUCTIONS

This recipe can be used for Melt and pour Soap. If you are not conversant with this method, then read this step by step guide.

For a mixed cream coating, melt white Melt and Pour Soap base and mix it up with a whisk for a fluffy coating.

Then for textured cream coating, you can dollop it onto the hardened soap.

3. Easy DIY Avocado Oil Soap

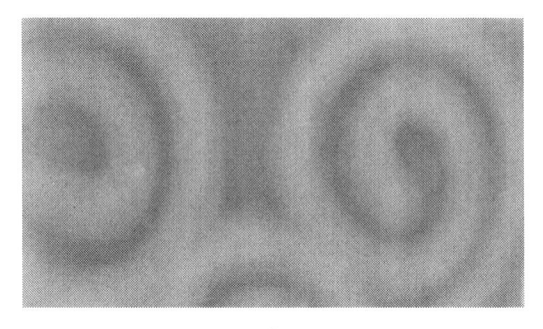

Not only that, this avocado oil soap is stunning to look at, but it also includes olive oil, coconut oil, and other skin-friendly ingredients. Lemongrass and sweet orange give it a lovely fragrance, and while it takes a few measures to achieve this stunning marbled look, it certainly worth the effort. You're going to get a soap that's not just great, but also, it's healthy.

RECIPES

- 10 of Avocado Oil - 90 gr. about 3.18 ounces.
- 30% of Coconut Oil - 270 gr. about 9.52 ounces.
- 30% of Comfrey Infused Olive Oil - 270 gr. about 9.52 ounces
- 30% of Palm Oil** - 270 gr. about 9.52 oz.
- Distilled Water - 326.1 gr. about 11.5 oz.
- 4.4 ounces of Lye - 125.4 gr.
- Water as % of Oils about 36.23
- Super Fat/Discount about 8%

Avocado Oil Soap Instructions

Step. 1

If you're planning to make this soap using the white soap curls, begin by making a Simple Homemade Soap batch.

Follow the instructions for making soap curls after the white soap has completed the insulation process.

Put the soap curls in the lined soap mold and set aside.

My normal size is the foundation recipe and is using 900 grams of oil. You can need a different mold to pump some excess soap base into it, based on how many curls you have and the size of your soap mold.

Step.2

Prepare a comfrey infusion using olive oil.

In a crockpot, put 1 cup of dried comfrey and fill with about 2 cups of olive oil. Place the crockpot on low heat for an hour, and switch it off afterward. Keep it covered overnight, then filter the herb the next day via a coffee filter.

Step.3

You should use either the soap making process for room temperature or the soap making method for cold processes.

When the soap hits a trace of light, you can add green oxide in the orris root and chromium. Make sure to mix correctly. Add the essential oils and blend properly. Pour the liquid soap carefully over the coils of the soap, taking care not to mess up the design. Cut the soap to maximize the appearance.

4.Adorable Homemade Bunny Soaps

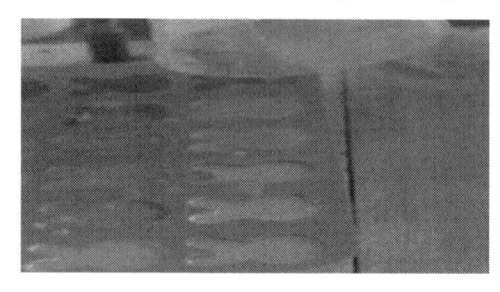

If you're searching for something special for Easter, or just a sweet little soap to decorate the children's bathroom, these little bunny soaps will capture your attraction. They're easy to make and great to add to Easter baskets or make birthday presents as springtime. Make them in various colors-they are healthy for all skin types as well!

RECIPES
- Soap Dyes
- White Glycerin Soap Base
- Easter Themed silicon mold
- Clear Glycerin Soap Base

Tools Needed
- Milk Carton or Bar Soap mold- if you want to make bars

INSTRUCTION

Follow the instructions on how to melt on the white soap packaging.

If the white soap has been melted, apply the soap dyes.

Just pour it into your molds and freeze. If bubbling happens, you should sprinkle some Rubbing alcohol on the soap, and watch the bubbles vanish. You can even layer various colors and work fast because until they are firm, the layers won't bind well.

5. Colorful Sunflower Goat Milk Soap

Sunflowers are perfect for adding glow and cheering to every room ... including bathroom. This is why I enjoy these little sunflower soaps made of goat's milk. They're also colorful and will give a lovely appearance to your bathroom immediately.

RECIPES
- 12 ounces of coconut oil
- 15 ounces of olive oil
- 13 ounces of other oil - lard, sustainably-sourced palm oil, fat, vegetable shortening, or another comparable oil
- 13 ounces of goat milk
- 6 ounces lye known as 100% sodium hydroxide
- 1-ounce of essential oils (optional)
- additives - lavender flowers or oatmeal, (this is optional)

INSTRUCTIONS

You have to freeze your goat's milk soap a day before you make your goat's milk recipe. It's not good enough to have it cold, and it has to freeze. You should put in the freezer zip-top containers and leave them there until you need them. Per bag is pre-measured at 13 ounces, and they are ready to use.

1. Then, a large glass or stainless-steel bowl is required. (Avoid using plastic, as it will carry odors.) Place this in a bigger bowl or sink and fill the outer bowl with cold water and freeze about half full, so it's very cold. Place your frozen chunks of milk into the inside bowl.

2. Add the lye very steadily, then squish it cautiously into the milk. For this stage, a potato masher in-oxidable-steel works very well. Start adding the lye until all of it is added. It is not going to get hot or even warm. Don't think about it. If the ice melts in the outer bowl, fill it again. It has got to be cold. It's normal whether the milk turns to light brown, or even white. If it gets dark brown, then you have to start again. At this stage, the milk is burned. The sugars in the milk are very reactive, so they need to be held very cold to prevent burning. And if you detect a smell of ammonia, this is also normal-just keep doing it. The scent will disappear as it settles.

3. Hold it on ice until the lye/milk is full until you have the oils ready. Use a kitchen scale to weigh the oils. Mix the oils and heat them gradually until it is roughly 110 °-125 ° F.

4. Pour the lye/milk mixture carefully into the oils slowly, when the oils are ready. For the first 5 minutes, stir by hand and use a stick

(immersion) blender to let it get a trace. If you have never made soap before, it gets very thick here, just like pudding. Add the essential oils and any ingredients when it comes to a trace, and put it into the mold.

5. Wait for 24 or more hours, extract from molds, and cut if necessary. Wait 3-4 weeks, turn it around so much that both sides become open to sunlight. To make sure it is done and ready to use (the optimal pH is between 8-10), you can measure the pH with test strips or use the traditional "press your tongue to it" process. If you feel some sort of tingling on your tongue, it isn't ready yet, and if used at this stage, it would be too hard on your face. Wrap it when it's thoroughly done.

6. Homemade Chocolate Soap

This is an easy soap to make. You could mold this in a soap mold or make it into a bar, which looks more suitable for chocolate, don't you think? I can add some sprinkles or anything to make it lovely. This cocoa butter, shea butter, and so many other excellent ingredients make it smell pleasant and give important health advantages to your skin.

Chocolate Soap Recipe

- 1-2 Tablespoons unsweetened cocoa powder
- 1/2 tsp cocoa butter
- 1/2 cup goat's milk powder
- 1/2 tsp mango butter or shea butter
- 1 tsp olive oil
- 2 Tablespoons chocolate fragrance oil
- 2 lb. clear coconut melt and pour soap base

INSTRUCTION

Melt the base of butter and soap. Add olive oil, take away from heat, then allow to cool slightly. Add the milk powder and mix well until no lumps are present. Add olive oil and cocoa powder until it achieves the desired color and smell. Pour it into molds. Release from the mold when soap hardens.

7. Coffee And Cream Soap

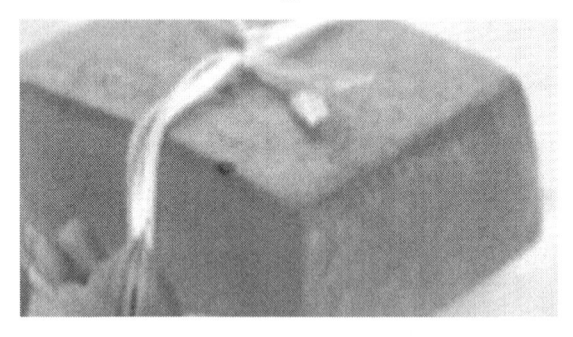

Coffee is gorgeous to look at and smells lovely. With newly ground coffee, vanilla, and powdered milk, you are sure to love rising to this soap daily, and it's lovely enough to decorate your bathroom for exclusive guests.

This glycerin soap recipe is meant for coffee lovers in your home. Its scents are like fresh coffee when you use it and has a deep brown color.

RECIPES
- 4z. bar melt and pour soap
- One teaspoon ground espresson
- One teaspoon powdered milk
- 10 drops coffee fragrance oil

INSTRUCTION
Melt the soap in a medium saucepan over low heat until it has liquefied. Remove from fire, mix in ground espresso, powdered milk, and oil of coffee fragrance. Pour into mold and allow it to settle for three hours or until it is hard.

8. Homemade Color Block Soap

These small soap bars have color blocks great to match any bathroom decor. They are not only fantastic for your skin, but they are also good for adding the elegant touch to your kitchen or shower. You can produce them in a soap mold – or you can find other items to shape them into – and you can pick the colors you like to suit your bathroom decor.

INSTRUCTIONS

RECIPES
- soap base
- soap dye
- essential soap oils

Tools:
- soap mold
- glass measuring cup
- knife + cutting board
- spray bottle of rubbing alcohol

1. Slice the soap base block to little one-inch cubes. Put four in a glass measuring cup and drop it for a minute and a half into the microwave, or until the soap is fully melted.

2. Put a few drops of mineral oil and some pigment and then stir the mixture.

3. Tilt the mold's edge up and pour the soap in to fill the corner.

4. Wait for the soap to settle for about 20 minutes, and then melt four more cubes. Repeat the same process except that this time put your blocks at the corner with your first soap sheet. Pour in enough soap to cover the other corner.

5. Get your second soap layer settle and then repeat for your final one.

6. Melt, mix, and pour.

7. Take a knife, and slice the soap into smaller chunks of one inch. Melt four into a measuring glass cup. Put essential oil and soap coloring in your pick, then mix.

8. Tilt the mold to an elevated level, so that all the liquid soap covers one corner. That will show you color diagonal lines in your soap.

9. Spray rubbing alcohol on the first layer of soap to help remove any bubbles. Put a few more alcohol spritzes to get rid of unwelcome air bubbles.

9. DIY Lavender Soap With Goat's Milk

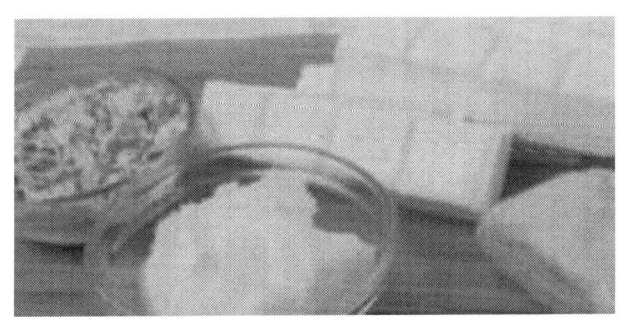

These little soaps include lavender, oatmeal, and goat's milk, all perfect for your hands. They are still very beautiful, painted with oats all over, and they smell wonderful. You can quickly mold these or use a cupcake pan to make tiny round soaps that are good to offer as presents or decorate your vanity in the bathroom.

1. **RECIPES**
- soap base
- soap dye
- essential soap oils

Tools:
- soap mold
- glass measuring cup
- knife + cutting board
- spray bottle of rubbing alcohol

2. RECIPES

- ½ tsp of Red Raspberry Seed Oil
- 2 cups of Goat Milk Soap Base
- 15 drops of Lavender Essential Oil
- ¼ cup of Shea Butter
- 3/8 cup of Rolled or Steel Cut Oats, divided (¼ cup + 1/8 cup)
- ¼ cup of Coconut Oil

3. RECIPES

- Measuring Cups
- Measuring Spoons
- 13"x9" Baking Pan
- Waxed Paper
- Double Boiler or Microwave
- Large Bowl
- Spoon
- Measuring Cup
- Measuring Spoons
- Spatula
- Cutting Board
- Knife
- Cookie Cutter or Soap Mold

INSTRUCTION

1. With a wax paper, Line a 13" x 9" baking pan and set it aside.
2. Get your goats milk soap base from the box and slice it into 1-inch cubes. Melt the base of the goat's milk soap in a double boiler or microwave until melted. When using a microwave, heat up for 45 seconds, mix, repeat until fully melted. Stir constantly until melted when using a double boiler.
3. Melt together the coconut oil and the shea butter in either a double boiler or microwave until melted. When using a microwave, heat up for 45 seconds, mix, repeat until fully melted.
4. Put this mixture melted into a big bowl.
5. Attach the molten goat milk soap base, and 1/4 cup rolled oats to the mixed coconut oil/shea butter combo; stir.

6. Add essential oil in lavender and seed oil in red raspberry; mix until smooth.
7. Pour the mixture into your wax paper bowl. Before the soap dries, cover with leftover oats and scatter the oats uniformly over the soap mixture.
8. Let the soap cool off, and remove the wax paper soap.
9. Put the soap on a cutting board and cut it into bars with a sharp knife or using cookie cutters for shapes.
10. If you have a cookie-cutter, you might need to cut the form out of the cookie-cutter that does not cut the soap cleanly.

Note: you can use the mold for this if you wish to do so.

10. Adorable DIY Lollipop Soaps

You can use those nice little lollipop soaps with a white soap base or transparent glycerin soap. Think of a way to get your children washed for dinner! They would love these soaps, and if you want to add any variety of items to make them more colorful, you can make them have several colors, like dried roses, confetti, or all kinds of other decorations.

RECPICES
- Lollipop sticks.
- clear glycerin soap base or white soap base
- Lollipop candy
- Mold.
- Food coloring
- Fragrance oil.

INSTRUCTION

First, have a strong base of Glycerin Melt, then Pour Soap. Then slice off 2-3 blocks of soap and place the soap in an old container. Bring in a Microwave after that. Leave in about 10-15 sec.

Stir in the fragrance, oil, and food coloring and scent of your choice for children when melted, and have mold ready for pouring in.

Let the soap sit about 5-10 min in the freezer. Pop-out mold and put in a lollipop stick. Be cautious, since this soap is small.

11. Homemade Pumpkin Vanilla Swirl Soap

It gives a yummy scent and looks great. This is a cold method and is somewhat different from melting and pouring, and it may take a little bit longer. Such bars are amazing once they're finished, and make wonderful presents during the holidays.

RECIPES

Liquid & Lye Portion:
- 4.19 ounces (119 grams) lye (6% super fat)
- 8 ounces (227 grams) distilled water

Oil Portion (30 ounces total):
- 16 ounces (454 grams) of olive oil (53%)
- 8 ounces (227 grams) of coconut oil (27%)
- 3 ounces (85 grams) of sunflower oil (10%)
- 3 ounces (85 grams) of cocoa butter (10%)

INSTRUCTION

1. Make it according to soap making general cold method. Mix in 2 ounces canned pumpkin at light trace.

2. Measure around 1/3 of the batter in a medium plastic tub (you may use a big recycled yogurt jar) Add in 1 tablespoon of pure vanilla, and 20 to 30 drops of essential oil clove. (Adjust according to your taste for scent) Pour the pumpkin soap halfway into the paper-lined parchment mold, apply the vanilla spice layer next, and top with the remaining of the pumpkin soap. Cover for two or three days and let it stay uninterrupted.

3. This soap requires a lengthier dry period than others, but don't panic if it first appears too soft. When unmolded, let the soap log hang out in the air for a couple more days before slicing to bars to allow plenty of room for solidifying.

12. DIY Rose Petal Soaps

You could see the rose petals via the soap base, and you get a beautifully scented soap that feels as lovely as it appears when you apply rose essential oils too. These also are relatively quick to produce. Simply add dried rose petals – or any flower you like – to the base of the soap when you shape it, and they come out lovely every time.

RECIPES

- An all-natural soap base.
- Beet Juice for coloring if needed
- Dried herbs and flowers of your choice (press the rose petals in a book for some days before using)
- your selection of essential oils (You can use Rose and Lavender)
- Soap Mold of your choosing

INSTRUCTION

1. Slice the base of the soap into tiny pieces and put it in a saucepan over hot water to melt. It may also take about 30 seconds to microwave the base on high.

2. Mix in your preference for essential oils. 1-2 drops are more than sufficient; the oils are strong. Be careful to mix steadily.

3. Put the petals at the base of the soap pot, then pour over the base. Use one of your flowers that stems from pushing down the petals into the base as they appear to float up.

4. To place flowers in the bar, you may do a layering strategy by pouring a thin layer of foundation, letting it dry for around 20 minutes, and then adding more flowers. Repeat until you get the perfect look.

5. If you choose to color the base of your soap, apply a tiny amount of beet juice, which will provide a pinky tint to the soap. To hurry up the process a little bit, you can put it in the fridge. They will be pretty great and easily come out of the molds. When they don't, then let them calm off a bit longer.

13. Handmade Lemon And Rosemary Soap

This rosemary and lemon soap is great for cooking, or you might even use it to decorate the vanity of the bathroom. The dried rosemary renders it very beautiful, with a nice lemony fragrance. Making soap, which can be made into bars or shaped in your favorite shape by pouring it into a soap mold, is easy.

RECIPES

- 1-pound melt and pour soap
- Four teaspoons grapeseed oil
- One teaspoon lemon essential oil
- One teaspoon dried rosemary
- Pyrex glass measuring cup
- Soap mold
- Soap Mold of your choosing

INSTRUCTION

1. Cut melt and pour the soap into small chunks. Melt in the microwave at 30-second intervals until melted. Stir between intervals.

2. Add grapeseed oil and stir. Let cool until it just starts to thicken. Add dried rosemary.

3. Add lemon essential oil. Add a drop of yellow food coloring if desired. Let sit until the top just starts to get a film on it. Pour into the mold and let sit until cool.

14. DIY Tie Dye Soap

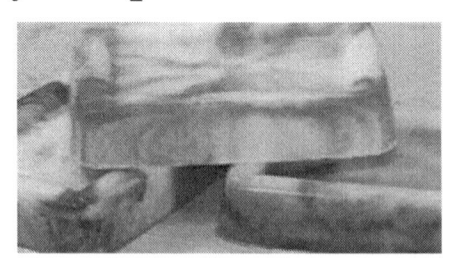

They are so sweet and colorful, and a perfect way to spice up the bathroom for a teenager. You may shape it into bars or signs of love, or anything you want. Also, they are a melt and pour soap, so they're easy to produce, and you can add any essential oils you like to give you the perfect fragrance.

RECIPES

- Small stick, toothpick or straw
- Melt and Pour Soap Base
- Liquid Soap Colorants
- Microwave Safe Bowl
- Molding Tray
- Knife
- Small Spray Bottle that is filled with Rubbing Alcohol (this is Optional

INSTRUCTION

1. Put your Melt & Pour Soap base on a flat surface, and slice it into 1-inch cubes with your knife. For two full bars of soap, split it about ten cubes.

2. Put your cut cubes in your bowl and put them in the microwave for 35 seconds. Take from the microwave after the process is full and give it a fast stir to ensure all the cubes are melted down to a liquid. Now is a perfect moment, should you like to add any essential oils. I'd just apply some lavender to him.

3. Position your molding tray on a flat surface and apply a drop of red and green to the base of the mold.

4. Then pour your soap into the molds, easily filling every cavity up to the rim.

5. When your molds have been filled, take your soap color and drop in red, blue, green, and yellow paint and easily start spinning the pattern around with your stick/straw.

6. You may note that the color starts to fall to the bottom, and then rises to the top. At the bottom, this produces a tie-dye effect.
7. Spritz the tops of the soaps use rubbing alcohol to get rid of the air bubbles Enable at least 2 hours of sitting in the mold.

15. Cute Jewelry Box Soaps

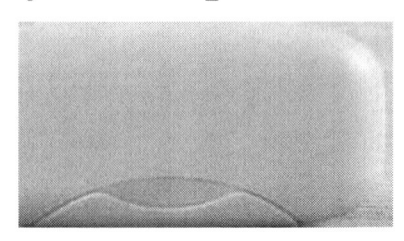

You can use a cardboard jewelry box that you can use to mold soap into bars and produce beautiful looking decorative soaps. You can use the glycerin soap with the fish embedded, which is easy to do. You could put anything that would suit your bathroom furnishings, and kids are going to love using soaps bars that have little creatures in them.

Tools
- metal cheese shredder
- cutting board
- double-boiler pan
- knife
- plate
- scissors

RECIPES
- jewelry boxes
- 1 to 2
- ribbons
- wax paper
- 1 to 2 tablespoons coconut oil
- clear glycerin soap
- tablespoons of oatmeal
- little plastic toys (optional)
- inexpensive perfume or cologne (optional)
- white bar soap
- 1 to 2 tablespoons of lavender or rosemary
- wrapping paper
- tape

INSTRUCTION

You should make a bar of clear glycerine soap with plastic fish inserted inside for the kids. (They're going to bath and wash just to get at the fish.) And make the adults have a scented oatmeal soap. Cardboard jewelry gift boxes for producing the soap may be used as forms. Once you are done, use the checkboxes for packaging your soaps and offering them as presents.

Step 1: Cut Glycerin Soap

Split the soap glycerol into small strips. It needs one soap bar per piece of jewelry.

Step 2: Put the soap slices in the top pan of a double boiler

Step 3: Heat up to Melt

Fill to halfway the base of the double boiler with water. Melt the top pan over the dish. Glycerin soap melts much quicker than normal soap.

Step 4: Line the Box

Cut the wax paper to fit, enabling you to line the interior of the jewelry cases, ensuring that the edges stretch outside the box. Using your fingertips to scatter a thin coconut oil layer across the wax cover. This can easily make the soap slip off the wax paper during refrigeration.

Step 5: Pour half once the soap has melted into the box with the lined jewelry. Let it sit for 2 minutes before the toy figurines are added. Often use glycerin soap when applying plastic figures to wash, as it is clear.

Step 6: Add-Ins Optional

Let settles for some minutes, put the pan of soap back on the double boiler, so it doesn't harden.

Step 7: Top It Off

Pour over the plastic figurines the leftover soap, be cautious not to overfill it, before it falls over the bottom of the jewelry case. Let sit and harden for 10 minutes before heading to a comfortable spot.

Step 8: Remove from Box

When the soap has dried, extract by rolling up the sides of the wax paper from the jewelry case. Peel the wax paper gently away from the wash, and seal it in a fresh sheet of wax paper.

Step 10: Gift Wrap

Wrap the soap into a beautiful paper and put it back in the package. Decorate with more paper packaging or a ribbon.

CHAPTER 6

All Natural Carrot Soap Recipe Using Real Carrots

Natural Carrot Soap Recipe

A small batch of natural carrot soap with carrot puree to add bright yellow color. It produces five to six bars of soap.

Equipment

- Measuring spoons
- Digital Kitchen Scale
- Soap mold(s)
- Digital temperature gun or you can use a thermometer)
- Immersion blender
- Stainless steel pan
- Heat-proof jug for the lye-solution
- Rubber spatula
- Small sieve (strainer)
- A large bowl

RECIPES

- Lye water
- 64 g Sodium hydroxide
- 50 g Carrot purée - 3 Tbsp
- 100 g Distilled water

Solid oils

- 59 g Shea butter
- 140 g Coconut oil (refined)

Liquid oils

- 30 g Castor oil
- 225 g Olive oil

Add after Trace

- 9 g Essential oil (Optional) - 2

INSTRUCTIONS

1. Make purée with carrots. The quantity you would need is about half of a medium-sized carrot for this recipe. However, you can prepare and

cook an entire one, just in case. Peel the carrot, then slice it as if for a meal you were going to make boiled carrots. Simmer up soft in hot water, then extract with a slotted spoon from the bowl. Blend using immersion blender into a purée. You should retain the water in which the cooked carrots are used to produce the lye solution, but first, make sure they cool it to room temperature.

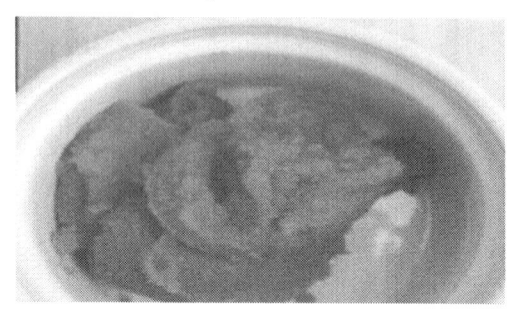

2. Prepare yourself. Cover in long-sleeves, trousers or long tops, and shoes with a closed shoe. Wear eye protection, like goggles and latex gloves, when using lye or the soap batter.

3. Lye (Sodium hydroxide) particles should be dissolved in water. Pour the lye crystals in water in an airy place, and mix well. You should do this outside because of the steam that will inevitably come off. It's not nice to breathe it in this, so prevent this by holding the jug away from you.

4. When mixed and the steam has started to disperse, add the carrot purée and mix well gently. The lye solution helps to break any residual purée fibers. The color is not impaired, either.

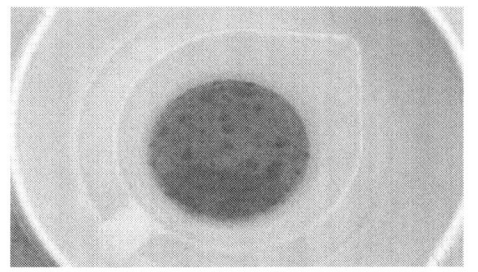

5. To cool, leave the lye-solution in a clean, shallow water basin, or sink. Ensure children and pets are unable to get to it.

6. Melt the strong oils at very low heat in an in-oxidable/stainless steel pan. Take off from the heat when melted, and put on a potholder. Pour the oils into the mixture and mix.

7. Measure lye-water levels and oils. You should try to cool each of them to about 100 ° F/38 ° C. You don't have to be on the spot, so you're aiming to keep them at the temperature or cooled slightly.

8. When you have taken them off, bring your gloves and goggles back on. Pour the lye solution over a sieve and into the oils pan. The filter will trap some unwanted carrot pieces and some undissolved lye. Dispose of the pieces you get.

9. Put the immersion blender into the pan and mix the mixture with it switched off. Take it to the middle of the pan, then grab it onto the bottom of the pan with both of your hands and blitz it for only a few seconds. Switch it off and mix the soap batter, using the blender like a knife. Repeat until the paste thickens up to 'Trace.' That is where the batter makes traces on the surface that can be seen. At first, consistency should be like thin custard, but it will easily thicken, so be sure to work fast at that point.

10. Should you like to add the essential oil as an alternative, mix it in at this stage. Pour in and mix softly until mixed completely.

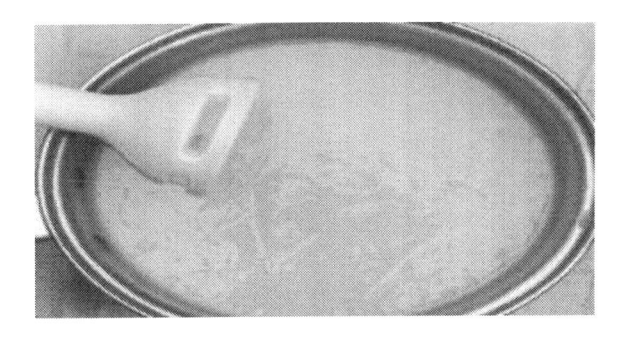

11. You can use all kinds of molds, but you should use a simple design. Wrap it in baking paper to prevent the soap from sticking through. The flaps on both sides are meant to support in bringing out soap bar. Nonetheless, you can use the silicone choice or certain mold forms.

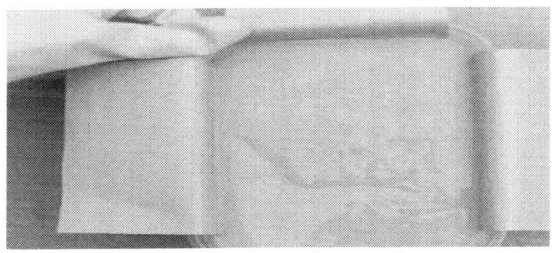

12. Pour the soap into the mold and put it on a heat-resistant surface. Keep the soap in the mold for two days or more. A week could be even better because this is originally quite a soft soap. Soap recipes that are strong in extra virgin olive oil appear to start soft and become very hard during the solidifying process.

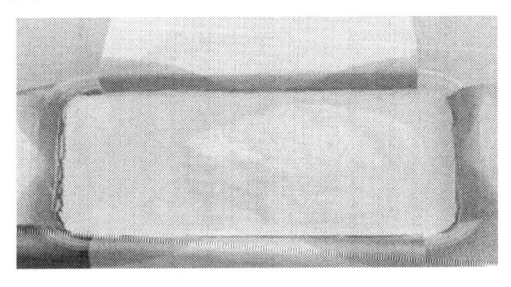

13. You should take the soap out after the period has elapsed, then slice it into bars. Use a regular kitchen knife and just pause to let the soap stay

for a couple more days in case you notice the soap is sticky. It is an olive oil heavy soap, so it has a lot of water content. At first, it will be sticky and soft, but it will harden with time.

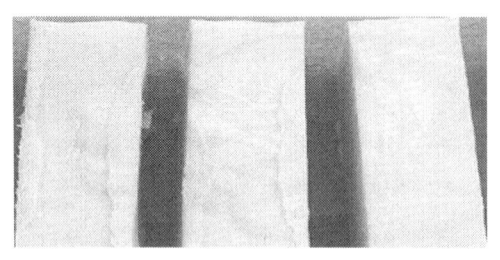

14. Let the bars solidify for six weeks after removing them. Solidifying involves keeping the bars spread out of direct sunlight and in an airy spot, on a covered surface. This makes complete evaporation of the extra water content. It also calls for the hardening of the bars. Upon cutting them, you might notice that your soap bars look a little sticky or muddy. That happened to one of my sets, so I left it like that. The bars became solid, nice, hard, and dry with time.

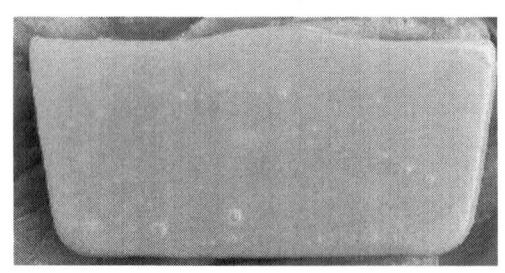

15. Your soap will have up to two years of shelf-life once it is made.

List of Soap-Making Methods

1. Cold Process

This is the most prevalent form of soap production. Cold process soap turns out to be hard and can last a long time. This process includes the application of fatty acids and lye, commonly known as sodium hydroxide. The fatty acids can be derived from virtually any oil or fat, including certain cooking oils and animal fats. Where the correct amounts of salt, sodium hydroxide, and fatty acids are combined, a mechanism called saponification would begin.

These ingredients are mixed at extremely high temperatures and only granted several weeks of cure. This method requires the hardening of the soap, which can be cut into bars. Only note, you have to prevent touch with lye on the skin.

The usage of protective equipment such as helmets, boots, long sleeves, and other appropriate garments is necessary for safety purposes.

A chemical reaction happens as the fat and lye mix. The reaction neutralizes the lye, such that usage on the body is safe. It takes on cleaning properties when the fat solidifies, to lift dirt free.

2. Hot Process

This soap-making approach is a more modern variant of the way of producing cold process soap. An inexperienced soap manufacturer should not perform the soap making process. It uses fatty acids and lye, much like the way of producing soap from the cold process. Yet, instead of boiling the ingredients and allowing them to harden for weeks, all the ingredients are combined and processed at very high temperatures to get rid of the water. The soap is allowed to cool down and is then ready for use.

3. Melt and Pour Soap

This is a simple way to make soap and good for beginners and kids. It involves using a pre-made soap as a base for the soap. A simple soap can be used with or without fragrances, colors, or other chemicals. The base of the soap is melted, and you can apply ingredients such as spices, colors, natural oils, scent powder, or shimmer to the surface. The following step, once mixed, is to pour the base into soap molds where it's allowed to harden. You will do it until the soap has solidified.

4.Rebatching or Hand-Milled

Rebatching is just another easy way to produce soap. It is like modifying soap. You can use old bits of soap or a bar of soap for this process, cut it down and put it on the stove in some water to enable it to liquefy. You may then apply new ingredients to the soap when it has melted. Using additives such as spices, essential oils, colorants, and fragrance oils may personalize the fragrance and other products. Then pour the soap into molds and allow it to harden again. When solidified, the soap is ready for use.

Considerations

Making soap can be an exciting and satisfying experience. There are lots of recipes and methods available for producing soap, so you need to do some work to determine what kind of soap you are interested in making. Beginners prefer using a melt and pour process since producing soap is a simple and inexpensive way. And this does not require lye use, which may theoretically be harmful. This process often doesn't require much time to produce. You can conveniently modify the soap with colors, scent, and also names and amusing phrases while producing soap. Add fun things that will make it look perfect. You may add things, anyone, in the house needs. Everybody may have their own specially made soap bar, even the kids.

The soap dye can be used in most craft shops. You should purchase natural pigments to color your soap too. This is a perfect way to render the soap desirable both in terms of quality and esthetics—the Skin benefits from spices, nutrients, salts, sugar, oatmeal, and even essential oils. For starters, sea salts help to exfoliate and reduce inflammation.

Explanation And Processing Of Hand Milled
Hand-Milled Soap Recipes

Either slow cooker or oven-roasting bag process may be used to produce either of those recipes. They all start with 1 to 2 pounds (454 to 908 g) freshly grated soap but can be raised to make larger batches.

Three-Layered Soap

This soap combines clay, activated charcoal, and ground walnut shells into a slim (2 pounds or 908 g) loaf-shaped washing and exfoliating cup.

RECIPES
28 ounces (794 g) of grated soap
4 to 6 ounces (113 to 170 g) of liquid

Additives

1 to 2 tbsp (5 to 10 g) of ground walnut shells

1 ounce (14 g) of essential oil or fragrance oil

One tbsp (9 g) kaolin, bentonite, or French green clay. One tbsp activated charcoal—a little goes a long way

INSTRUCTION

1. Pour and mix the liquid onto the shreds and melt the soap using the process of a slow cooker or roasting pan.
2. Mix in the scented oil until it has fully cooled. Divide the mixture into three parts.
3. Mix the walnut shells into the first part. Mix the clay into the second part. Add the charcoal to the third part.
4. Layer per portion of the mold. Lightly scoop or pour the soap into the mold for a pleasing look to the layers and smooth each coating afterward. You have it put aside to cool and harden.

Swirled Hand-Milled Soap Bars

With hand-milled soap, some swirling is possible, particularly if the soap isn't really old and has sodium lactate in it. You may use this process in individual molds.

RECIPES

1 lb (454 g) of freshly grated soap

(28 g) of sodium lactate

(57 to 85 g) of liquid of choice

Additives

½ teaspoon of red mica

0.5 ounce (14 g) of fragrance oil or essential oil

½ teaspoon of purple mica

½ teaspoon of yellow mica

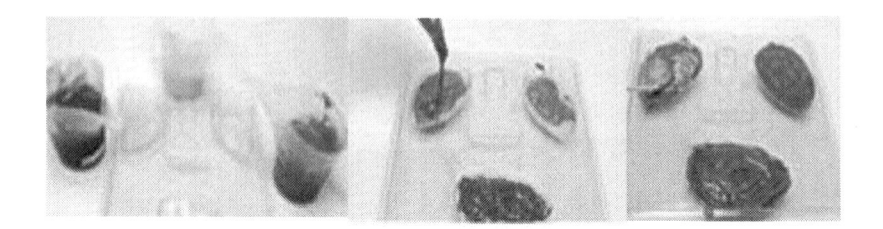

INSTRUCTION

1. Pour the liquid onto the shreds and heat the soap using a form of slow cooking or roasting bag on the oven. When completely melted, split the mixture into three parts.

2. Apply the mica yellow to one section, the mica red to the second portion, and the mica purple to the sixth. Mix well.

3. Pour a little bit of growing color into mold(s), but one color beside each and top of others.

Melt-and-Pour Soap

Types of Melt-and-Pour Bases

Remember, all soap contains these necessary ingredients—lye (sodium hydroxide), water, and oils. Melt and pour soap is the same. On the ingredient list for your soap base, it is possible to see ingredients such as "water, sodium hydroxide" or "sodium laureate."

Other ingredients are put into the base to enable it to melt, make it lather, or add other taste qualities.

Other ingredients you may see are:
• Sorbitol (sugar-derived alcohol and Glycerin aides the soap base to be clear.
• Propylene glycol helps the soap in melting.
• Sodium Lauryl Sulfate (SLS), detergents, foaming agents, and surfactants) helps the soap to lather, clean, and rinse fully.

Some ingredients give moisturizing and other advantages for the skin as well as label appeal. In addition to the bases with specific additives, there are also bases formed for special purposes.

Some of the most popular are:

• **Suspension base:** A much thicker base that helps additives stay suspended in the melted soap instead of sinking to the bottom.

• **Low-sweat base:** Formed to imitate cold process soap more firmly, a low-sweat base has a lower glycerin content, so it is less inclined to sweating like normal melt-and-pour soaps.

• **Natural base**: A base formed without any soaps or surfactants to be as natural as feasible.

• **Unique ingredient base:** Many specialty bases are available with unique ingredients.

Notwithstanding the base you use, melt-and-pour soap allows you just to melt the soap, fragrance, add your color, and additives, and pour it into a mold. It's available to use as soon as it cools and solidifies.

Primary Method for Making Melt-and-Pour Soap

Follow these steps for perfect soaps.

1. Start with your selected melt-and-pour soap base. Cut up and measure enough soap to make the amount of bars you want, with a few extra for waste adjustment. The smaller the soap chunks are, the more quickly they will melt.

2. Put the soap chunks into a heatproof bowl and melt them in the microwave in 30- to 45-second bursts, mixing in between. The soap will start to melt at about 49°C to 54.5°C.

3. Continue heating and melting gradually. Cautiously watch over the soap to make sure it does not start to boil. Continue to melt and stir in about 30- to 45-seconds until the soap is entirely melted. The rest of the soap chunks should melt as you mix the soap and add other ingredients. If not, give the soap another 5 to 10 seconds in the microwave to complete the melting, or just remove the unmelted chunks.

4. While the soap melts, measure the fragrance oil. What you need is about 3 percent of the soap's total weight. This batch makes 1 pound of soap or four 4-ounce bars, so use 0.5 ounces fragrance oil.

5. When the soap is fully melted, mix in the colorant, being cautious not to produce too many bubbles in the soap.

6. Once the melted soap cools to about 55°C, gently stir in the fragrance oil.

7. Once all additives are mixed in, at that instant, pour the soap into the molds. If the soap starts to harden too much to pour easily, reheat it for a few seconds to make it more liquid.

8. spray the soap using rubbing alcohol to remove any bubbles that may have formed.

9. Let the soap sit, cool, and solidify. This should take an hour or so. To rush the process, it's okay to freeze the soap.

10. As soon as the soap cools and hardens, it's set to unmold and use.

Layered Melt-and-Pour Designs

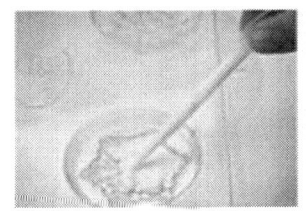

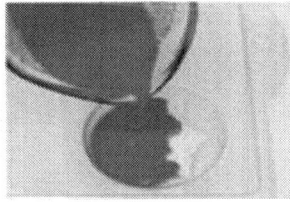

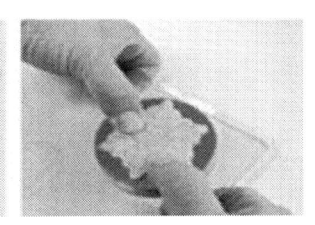

Because it cools and solidifies so quickly, melt-and-pour soap allows for easy coating. Most single-cavity mold designs have set up areas that help themselves for a plastic pipette to pour or pip in the molten soap. The secret to pouring the soap hot is to have its temperature about 65.5 ° C while pouring it into the mold. These molds enable you to create layered, multicolor, custom designs easily.

Basic Layered Soaps with Piped-in Designs

1. Melt 1 to 2 ounces of soap base and add a nonbleeding colorant or mica, if wanted.

2. With the soap still hot and fluid 65.5°C, pull the soap into the pipette and pipe the soap into the wanted part of the mold.

3. spray the soap using rubbing alcohol to eliminate any bubbles.

4. Let the piped soap cool and solidify.

5. Heat up and color the soap for the soap bar at the bottom. Spray the first piped soap using rubbing alcohol. This helps the layers stick to each other better.

6. When the second pour of soap cools to about (54.5°C), pour it into the mold.

7. Let the soap cool and solidify and gently unmold it. When you use silicone molds, the soap comes out easily. With plastic molds, use both thumbs to firmly, but slowly, remove the soap out of the mold. Freezing the soap for 15 to 20 minutes helps the soap remove easily from the mold, as well.

Embedding Botanicals

Natural botanicals should be applied to the melt-and-pour soaps, in addition to scent and color. They can add natural color, exfoliation, or simply aesthetic appeal. As the soap base has been made, melt-and-pour soap additives that don't stand up to touch with the lye perform well.

Mixing Botanicals Throughout

This is the easiest way to mix in botanicals, but the melted soap's fluid nature means more substantial additives sink to the bottom of the mold. To keep them thoroughly mixed, you wait till the soap solidifies to about 49°C, or you can use a suspension base.

1. Chop, measure, and melt your soap base.
2. Mix in the fragrance oil and color, if desired.
3. Mix in the botanicals. If using a suspension base, pour at 54.5°C or so. Try to stir gently until the soap cools to between 40.5°C and 43°C to pour into the mold if you are using a standard base.

CHAPTER 7

How Much Money Can I Make Online Selling Homemade Soap?

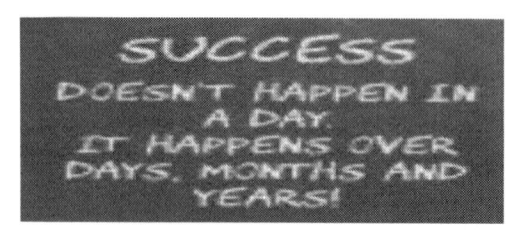

> SUCCESS DOESN'T HAPPEN IN A DAY. IT HAPPENS OVER DAYS, MONTHS AND YEARS!

A couple of Several factors determine the sum of money that you earn.

- Product appeal
- Way of selling
- Cost to make

To be able to advertise soap online effectively, it would require a lot of effort and research to see what works well and which items become the best and top sellers.

Product Appeal

Firstly, you should try to distinguish yourself from other sellers to build as much uniqueness as possible with your brand products and soaps.

People can pay more for organic soap produced with all-natural materials, with exclusive and unique fragrances, attractive packaging, and reasonable quality.

Way Of Selling

Another aspect would be how you decide to market the soap, as selling on Etsy maybe works better than selling soap on Amazon. Checking the multiple industries can take a while to see which does best.

You might also mix various marketing tactics such as selling soap on a variety of websites like eBay and Etsy when setting up a blog or website and use affiliate marketing to promote your home-made soap as well.

Cost To Make

That would be the most critical business aspect.

Until you can make money selling soap online, you should have an understanding of what the cost is to produce each bar of soap. This means you know whether you are going to be successful or not.

That is achieved by ensuring that product quantities are correct and documented, as well as the time it takes for you to produce it.

People typically start selling hand made soap as a hobby, so that they don't maintain reliable track of their time or blends to provide a particular scent. If you want a viable and productive company selling soap online, maybe you think you ought to move from hobby to corporation.

How To Sell Soaps You Have Made?

Manufacturing a product is only a portion of the process cycle necessary to generate real income. To make all of your efforts valuable, you need to find out a way to market the soaps you've made. There are a variety of techniques or tactics that you may use to sell your soaps. You have to remember to remain committed first of all, or else you won't have an easier time having customers to purchase your product. Everybody wants soap, so creating it is a smart idea. Just note to advertise the soap to the most significant degree possible so that customers realize its existence.

You are creating a platform for customers to buy soap from everywhere in the world. Soap is valuable because people are still trying out new things. The easiest way to advertise your soap on your website, social media accounts, or everywhere else is to tell customers that no animals have been hurt in the production process of this product or commodity.

The fact that all of the product is tested on livestock before being usable in the open market, soaps from large companies have undergone significant criticism in recent years. Notify all of your prospective buyers that your soap is all safe and that in manufacturing this product, you have not hurt any animals or the environment. When utilizing these communication tactics, you can attract a lot of people's attention or win more of your audience's heart to buy your product.

Create platforms on all major social networking websites to get your brand built online. Link all your accounts, and people learn about your soap. Link people to your profile on Facebook, Twitter, and Instagram so they can learn and know more about you and your product or brand. Write periodically during the day to keep all of your fans aware of your involvement. The easiest way to build more Facebook followers is to create an ad that reaches your specific or targeted audience.

For example, if your soap is more for women aged 30-50 than you can direct advertisements to specific individuals, invest a minimal sum of money into advertising, and you will get a lot of people to follow your message. On the leading social networking sites, make sure you use hashtags (e.g., #soap) at the end of any message you make. Hashtags let people learn about your life online. Use soap, laundry, and hygiene-related hashtags so that people interested in such topics can locate your brand or product.

Internet marketing isn't a limit. Speak to people you know regarding the soap products you made for them. This is a smart opportunity to indulge in a friendly chat with someone while you're in line at the supermarket, getting ready to buy a meal or somewhere that has other people. Let people learn, and where they can find your soap product.

Design business cards to send to customers, and they have to check your website later on when they get home to their device if you have spare time creating flyers on your hands and distributing them around your neighborhoods. If you may put a poster outside your establishment to advertise your latest product, ask nearby businesses to. Exposure is a crucial or most vital component of marketing a commodity or product. The more customers see it, the greater the possibility of having profits that you may have.

Contact nearby retailers to see if they will be involved in taking stock of your soap products. You should tell a company that your soap is increasing in popularity, and that keeping it in stock will be smart for them. Note the quality of other soaps and find out how high the brand will be paid for the sale. Establish a fair price for purchasing your soap over certain products that will help you to make money and still impress customers or buyers.

Price plays a major role in how much a product or commodity is doing in the store. Another thing you like to have is the corporate perspective on any soap line. Here's where you can explain the identity you want your business to portray to get more customers or buyers interested in purchasing your product. You may want to remember that, as opposed to a large company or organization, this is a soap commodity or product produced naturally by a person or a small group of people.

People of today's society want to support smaller companies, as opposed to large multinational corporations or firms. When you differentiate yourself from major corporations, you might start making loads of revenue and rise in popularity. Free samples can help with the selling of your product or items. Develop free samples every day to give to customers, and they can see if the soap is something they would want. You may want to carry with you some free samples and business cards and hand them around.

Selling soap effectively doesn't happen immediately. You have to be consistent with your actions, seek and be as positive or optimistic as possible before sales commence or begins. And if you let them think it's available can customers get involved in your soap. have in mind to build a commodity you'd and will routinely use. If you're not buying your stuff, it will make things appear terrible for customers market the company online and in person, as much as possible. Soap is a successful commodity capable of producing substantial income as everyone wants, and they are always in need of soap.

Selling Soap Legally & Regulations

When you want to take the risk of selling your hand-made soap online to raise money, it's important to know or to understand that soap regulations exist.

You will learn these otherwise you could get in trouble with the authorities. Any soap vendors have had unexpected inspections from the FDA because they used the incorrect terms in their ads and labeling.

Selling Homemade Soap Online: Pros and Cons

Let's analyses some of the positive and negative sides of attempting to market soap online to make money.

Pros (the good stuff)
- Simple ingredients
- Low cost or minimal capital to get started
- Standard kitchen equipment to be used
- Only a small space needed to get started

Cons (the adverse stuff)
- Easy to start but has lots of competition
- FDA regulations
- A lot of sales is required to earn or make income or more
- Time commitment

How You Can Market Your Handmade Soap Efficiently and Easily

Soap-makers manufacture their organic soap and other products outstandingly. As a general rule, much of their resources (time, money, and energy) are focused on making the best goods they might provide. Soap-makers always go the extra mile to ensure sure their formulae are correct, their products shine, and when it comes to materials, they get the most significant value for their money.

But all the hard work making quality goods won't bring them to you; that's what marketing is about!

Typically speaking, a soap company owner will invest 20 percent or less of their time manufacturing goods or performing duties relevant to development (such as purchasing inventory, formulating new items, etc.) the remainder of the time? All the money, honey! Then at the top of the list, make sure you sell your handmade soap like the future of your company relies on it (because it does!) Chances are you're a clever whip soap-maker (after all, you're here), so you don't know how to market your handmade soap! And you could be pushed in a lot of different directions and not know how to push on. It doesn't have to be that hard!

Use a Personalized Plan to Market Your Handmade Soap

For most soap-makers, the major missing element is a business strategy or tactic that maps out precisely where business activities will be centered, how to win in certain areas, and how to trim the fat. Let's see over the four critical measures for a successful marketing plan for homemade soap and other products.

Step 1: Prioritize Your Marketing Efforts

The explanation of why it still seems the campaign strategies are all over the place is because they are undoubted! Regardless of what the gurus claim, you ought to find out where the campaign strategies are and which ones take priority.

The first step to selling your home-made soap is to decide where your time, effort, and resources will be invested. As a general rule, I suggest, first and foremost, that soap-makers center marketing strategies in their own house. By your own home, what do I mean? They are all the communication channels you manage, including your platform, your email newsletter, and your forum. You don't want to spend all this time on constructing a house for anyone else!

In order of importance, you'll want to focus on marketing your hand-made soap and other products in these places:

- Your website (Soap making website that you own)
- Your email newsletter
- A blog or other platform of content marketing
- Various organic social media posting
- Various paid advertisement
- Other shiny objects/marketing stuff

The marketing target strategy would suit most soap-makers, although not all undertakings are the same. You might see a huge return on investment (ROI) with paid ads rather than social networking or with social media instead of blogging. You can notice that you are sparkling on video, and a YouTube channel will be a perfect marketing move for videos.

List all the different means or ways that you can sell your home-made soap and other products, and decide where you can concentrate your energies. Please consider the following:

- Can you outsource or hire help with you making use of this marketing strategy?
- Do you control the marketing effort?
- Is this marketing technique scaleable?
- Can you reach out to your customers using this method?
- Are you willing to learn how to use this marketing method?
- Does this marketing method seem easy and simple for you?

There's one thing that doesn't change: the email newsletter and website always come first. As a soap manufacturing company owner, they are things that you can completely control, and you don't want to place all the eggs in the basket place of others.

Step 2: Strategize Your Marketing Efforts

Now that you know where your marketing activities will be centered or targeted, you can narrow down each marketing strategy and think creatively on how to utilize it to your advantage.

The utmost thing that you should do is to set goals for every communication strategy that you use. Set one to three targets or priorities for each one that you have for using the type of marketing. For example, your objectives for the website could be to:

- Sell your homemade soap and cosmetics
- Help your customers love most of your products
- Tell the true story behind the success of the product, and give a valuable insight

This should make it crystal plain what you will be concentrating on while pursuing your home-made soap and makeup ads. In the case of the website, you realize that the website wants to turn guests into buyers, encourage a simple checkout procedure, and also upsell the goods to achieve the first goal.

Then, evaluate every single goal. But instead of "selling your handmade soap," the aim could turn into "selling 100 bars of handmade soap per month." That's one area that I love about SMART targets. (If you don't know what SMART targets are, they're Precise, Tangible, Realistic, Important, and Timeboxed.) Then put to paper how you're going to achieve the goal. You might want it to be weekly update, or monthly summary of income and loss.

Afterward, brainstorm ideas for reaching the goals under each one. If you aim to sell a hundred bars of handmade soap on your site each month, you can write down precise ideas to:

- Improve your copywriting
- Drive traffic to your website
- Optimize your checkout process
- Show off your products visually

You may always want to continue to direct your strategies to your audience as you examine various forms of selling your hand-made soap and cosmetics. Everybody that visits your website maybe with your brand in any type of stage.

- **Awareness:** They know your identity or what your products are all about.
- **Recognition:** They identify you for what you do, your mission, your vision, and what makes you distinctive.
- **Interest**: They are interested in trading with you.
- **Purchase:** They make transactions with their hard-earned cash for your products.
- **Repurchase:** They love your handmade goods enough to purchase it again.
- **Loyal:** They won't trade with any other brand again.
- **Influencer:** They will inform family and friends because people have to know about you and your product.

A new visitor isn't likely to fill up their shopping cart and press the order button on the website, for example. They are in the initial stages of the customer development process and are not yet ready to purchase. So, what can you do to make them step forward on that path?

Moreover, they don't have to get to know your company or hear your story when a new consumer gets on your website. Perhaps they're searching for advice on their previous order, answers to their questions, or a simple and painless way to reorder.

Ensure you customize any marketing campaign strategy that you have in the consumer life cycle to your aims and the various steps. Cover all of the bases! Once you complete this big, complicated cycle, you should have a blueprint for marketing to direct you along the way.

You'll use the marketing strategy to determine whether to pursue a new item (look, a new social networking platform!) or not and if the initiative you're putting forward is working with your strategy.

Is this starting to sound overwhelming?
Yes, I admit! When the marketing activities overtake you, it is time to put up a chopping block.

Do not cause fear of losing out (FOMO) to force you to stretch too thinly. I suggest focusing on your website, email update, and ONE other marketing technique if you are just beginning.

When you add a new marketing method to your plan and objectives, make sure to examine yourself saying:
- Are you feeling like you are ready to add to your schedule?
- Can you reach your buyers using this technique?
- Does this marketing technique relate to your brand's values, voice, and message?

Hold it on the shelf for later if you can't say yes to all three questions.

Which communication tool would you want to combine with your email newsletter and web site? Without understanding you, the company, and the target audience, nobody should tell you what's best. You should not let your attention be on other people's successful products or business. Ask yourself the three main questions about each marketing platform or technique, then seek to focus down on one.

Step 3: Put Your Marketing Into Action

Already, you know where your marketing activities will be centered, and you have a million suggestions about how to sell your hand-made soap. What next? Have the work completed, superhero!

Build a marketing plan, and you know precisely what you have to do to effectively fulfill your strategy and sell your homemade soap. As they say, it won't get done if it isn't planned.

Then concentrate on automating the performance of the operations and auditing. When each week you are receiving an email update with a new blog article, set up your email provider to pull the link from your RSS list. If you post every day on Facebook, plan your posts ahead of time and automatically let Facebook manage the rest.

You completely need accuracy and efficiency in your operations as you sell your homemade soap and cosmetics alone. Otherwise, you will be exhausted constantly, and none of it will ever be simple!

Step 4: Repeat

Since you've read up on how to sell your homemade soap and cosmetics, you're going to resent me for this next paragraph. It's time to begin from the top when you have got all lined together, operating in sync, and creating magic.

You know, marketing shifts as often as individuals alter what they experience. What succeeds today will not succeed next year or next month, or tomorrow at all. You must review and change your strategy periodically. I suggest you sit down quarterly for your marketing strategy (alongside your financial reports). Use it as an incentive to make changes, focus on what works, and analyze what does not work. Three months is the best period to send an honest commitment to a marketing strategy and see if it works for you.

If you slip off your marketing cart, shake the dirt off yourself, and climb back again. The greatest challenge in business for soap-makers is discovering how to sell their homemade soap and cosmetics. Maybe you're producing the most excellent selling soap in the whole wide world. If nobody cares about it, that's probably what your bottom line will show.

Let Us Go Further On How To Efficiently Market Your Soap products

The Online And Offline Soap-Making Marketing Strategy why does Your Business Needs Social Media Marketing!

Social networking marketing has been an important tool in the arsenal of both companies and organizations, with opportunities for relationship development, engaging with customers and grow sales like never before, and with information to prove it.

If you are not using social networking at all or your current strategy is not functioning as planned, now is the time for making a change.

You'll discover more than enough tips in this book to advertise your soap company successfully through the most popular social networking channels, including; **Pinterest, YouTube, Twitter, Instagram, and Facebook.**

The usefulness of social networking marketing is the product of the active establishment of professional partnerships with qualified customers and contacts.

This approach will help draw in and maintain loyal customers and contacts, which will allow sales reps to sell the soap products. This is a total reversal of an old marketing type. Around the same time, this approach is an environment that looks beyond the way conventional marketing operates; this open, two-way connectivities is essentially what billions of consumers around the environment expect from the businesses and products that they invest time and money on.

Decide which social networks you love most and will use

You are most inclined to focus on one or two social networks first because you are a large company with the resources to plow all the social networks at full steam. But not all social networking platforms can match the soap marketing target with what you're setting out to accomplish. Therefore, you ought to recognize which social networks are now "hanging out" your target audience.

Search and join Facebook-based groups so you can influence the top customers on your soap product and marketing.

To find the right way to advertise your soap goods, however, you need to experiment with a couple of social networking sites to help you get the best networking that suits your aim.

Define and review your priorities

Before you start posting your content on social media, you have to establish a target and strategy or guides to achieving them because they can help you make it a fact. Read the points below to help you.

- **Achievable:** Is your goal realistic to achieve? If you're just getting started, never target high when you were just starting a soap company (Particularly when you are first contemplating social media marketing seriously).

- **Measurable:** How do you think you achieved your goal? Which analytics tools did you use to monitor your progress?

- **Time Specific:** You will adhere to one overall target at a time and bring an emphasis on the soap marketing objective, e.g., "I plan to increase traffic on my online soap shop by 15 percent in the next three months."

- **Specific:** Be realistic about what you want to be doing. Want to start developing brand recognition? Would you like to develop a strong working partnership and increasing sales?

Handle complaints in the right way and Give outstanding customer service

Social media brings clients to the soap industry quickly and efficiently 24 hours per day and seven days per week. Customers should have fair access to you, so that is no more apparent than what can be perceived or defined as a change in customer satisfaction.

Social media absorbs uptime

Social media is becoming a significant resource for publicity and Marketing nowadays and should be done in a serious way.

Social media marketing which is also known as a paid advertisement

Several years back, social network marketing was seen as a perfect chance to reach out to target customers for free. But now, with growing demand and a cleverer sector, having paying ads distributed is all but unlikely.

The key with a ton of successful social networking advertisements is messaging that blends with a user's understanding of the site they feature on, mirroring the audience's sound and writing style as for free material, working seamlessly rather than disturbing it.

Reexamine returns on investment metrics

In some ways, the return on expenditure on social networking is not like traditional ads; you do not automatically want to focus on measurable benefits alone for a defined period of time. Consider initiatives such as awareness of brand soap company, social network traffic going to the website shop, word-of-mouth promotion, and growing consumer loyalty and engagement with current buyers. In the long run, they would both be fairly advantageous in terms of loads of income over a sustained period, instead of a short-term boost that would easily die-off.

Develop strong, significant relationships and Enjoy the ride
The more your name is acquainted with others on social media, the more likely they will identify you and pass on the correct message to their friends and relatives. If you want to encourage meaningful engagement with customers on a slow and steady road to creating lifelong loyalty, sales, and brand ambassadors, be honest, straightforward, up-to-date and authentic for all of your contacts.

Share a personal story and get the feedbacks tales from your customers
Every business and everybody, whether by text or by images, has a fantastic story; we are hard-wired to react to a compelling story. Using social networking as a location where customers will get much more acquainted with you and your company than simply showing the products or services you offer. In addition, persuade customers that you value their viewpoints and beliefs and become a business that they choose to invest directly, eventually leading to loyalty and purchasing. Aside from your own experiences, the consumers or consumers may also have interesting and informative tales about how you and the soap product work with their

lives, and maybe it's going to be more stimulating than the content that provides.

So let them tell you their stories through pictures, images, or email so that you can use them for content as part of your strategy. Doing this would encourage and please the customers involved, encourage them to spread the passion for your product, help build a more extensive market surrounding your soap products, and also act as strong, encouraging proof to many of how your brand has a beneficial impact on people's lives.

Address issues, be useful and share your experience
Placing the soap products as an authority is one of the most effective ways to impact social network users in building digital and emotional relationships for you. One of the best approaches to do this is to explore and illustrate the understanding of the challenges that you overcome when making soap products.

Promote your soap products and apply the 80 / 20 rule
While several of the social network advertisement posts aren't meant to be overtly advertising, promoting your soap product is what you're looking for and keeping consumers aware of. The 80/20 model is a straightforward approach to balance your social network output in a manner that puts you at the right side of your clients with one that is already utilized by certain businesses. It states that, with the sole purpose of enhancing interest, you should post non-promotional content 80 percent of the time of your relevant, valuable, or personable information, or related content linked to another site, and require the remaining 20 percent to become more

promotional. Just inside that 20 percent, there is a broad range of strategies, from subtle sales to more open sales, depending on how you think the consumer would react.

Make your soap pictures self-explanatory and powerful

The best photos to use on social media are those that draw attention, cultivate interest, excite, inspire excitement, or express a captivating image. If the photo represents an event important to your company or not, it doesn't matter; the key thing is to help encourage the kinds of feelings that you want consumers to connect to your soap brand.

Share a coupon code or an exclusive offer

Customers love exclusive offers, and pictures are a great way to show them dynamically and courageously.

Where appropriate, using words such as "special" and "limited time only" to complement these new soap marketing images to portray your goods as fresh with a forward-thinking and to ease the confidence of your customers in purchasing your soap items.

Facebook Marketing techniques

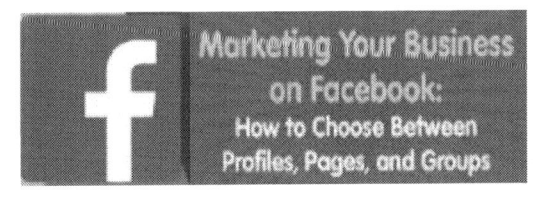

Facebook is the world's most-visited and most used social network, with over two billion users online. Your target audience is those using Facebook, and your target market is on Facebook. You can use these ideas to create, promote, and sell your business, as well as obtain highly engaged customers that will be buying your products from you.

Techniques for setting up Facebook business pages

Before you share anything on Facebook, it is advisable to build solid groundwork beforehand to help build up your online status perfectly and to satisfy customers when they buy your soap products.

Create and Develop a Facebook page or group instead of a personal profile

You need to create a dedicated Facebook account (group or page) to get the best out of what Facebook marketing has to offer for your company. Facebook Pages gives unique brand tools such as analytics, personalized tabs to display specifics of the product, and advertising technology you need to promote your soap business to the world.

Let your name be as short as possible on your Facebook page

If necessary, aim to keep your name short on your Facebook page because that would allow you to build Facebook advertisements if you believe it is appropriate to do so and respect Facebook's terms and conditions.

Fill in business info correctly and in detail

on one part of your Facebook profile, put in information on specifics of your products as much as you can, including location, Soap product numbers, contact details, Website (add many Links to the Website box by breaking them with commas), and links to other social networks.

Create an awesome Soap cover photo and add a call-to-action button

Facebook Page cover photos can be seen by everyone on Facebook, so use the medium to share the brand or message easily with one clear, high-quality picture. The perfect size is 851 x 315 pixels. If it is much less, Facebook will extend the picture dynamically, rendering it appear blurred. Cover picture options provide one compelling illustration that shows who you are and what you are doing, a collage of your products, a current offer, or a picture or testimonial provided by one of your followers. Essentially, the latter would really "please" the client, and ideally, they can spread the word to others. Keep users interested by changing the cover picture and profile image regularly-once a month is a perfect goal for targeting, but a seasonal shift is often common among brands.

Facebook Marketing Basics

since your Facebook Page is now looking exceptional and you're urging people to visit it, let's examine some ways that you can make the most efficient use of the platform, in collaboration with the content technique ideas.

Pin important posts

Facebook lets you pin a particular post to the top of your page's Timeline for a week. You can use this to feature important content and make it appear to visitors and fans who visit your page. All new status updates will be visible under the pinned post until it is unpinned (it elapses automatically when a week passes), at which point it will fall into its original chronological position. In particular, posts to think about when pinning include contents, special announcements, promotions, etc.

Boost clicks through call-to-actions but avoids "click-baiting."

To aid higher click-through rates from Facebook and other social media to your website and page, being precise about what you want your customers to do using a simple and straightforward call to action is a good idea, e.g., "Click here for further information [i.e., your link]." often, there are some times that those little clicks can show the contrast between a successful status and the unsuccessful ones.

Thank your newest fans

Write a special 'Thank You' note to greet new fans once a week, also naming them by name if there aren't so many-locate them via the "See Likes" button in the Admin Panel on your website. By doing so, the contact would have a personal touch and reflect well on the identity as a company that looks after the welfare of its customers. To promote more interaction on your profile, launch an initiative called "Customer of the Month." In therefore promoting one of your most loyal supporters, you implicitly inspire other supporters to participate further, so that they can earn the coveted title the next month.

Give the winner a small bonus for an extra reward. There are some free "Favorite of the Month" applications accessible via the search bar on Facebook, and premium ones with extra features if you're involved in deeper diving.

Create Facebook Offers

Facebook groups are a simple place to network with friends, improve relationships with existing consumers, or draw new ones-whether you're building your own or entering one of the millions that already exist. If you want to have the best out of groups concentrating on conversations regarding your preferred sector, your goal will be to put yourself as an authoritative figure: be involved, offer support, and be real, i.e., not based on sales. Your experience and reputation can be recognized with time, and it will continue to pique the attention of customers, maybe enough to make them want to buy your product or service.

Utilizing Facebook Groups to build your business

Facebook Groups are a great place to network with friends, improve partnerships with existing clients, or draw new ones-whether you're building your own or entering one of the millions that already exist. When you want to get the best out of groups engaging in conversations in your preferred sector, your objective will be to put yourself as an authoritative figure: be involved, offer support, and be real, i.e., not based on profits. Your experience and reputation should be recognized over time, and that will help pique the attention of customers, maybe enough to make them decide to try your product or service. One big market potential with small trade communities who rely on purchasing or selling all sorts of products and services is that most customers with built-up communities should be able to locate one for their city or region.

Search for a local group, seek how trade takes place there, and sell your products in a suitable manner.

Alternatively, once you build your community, it will act as a venue for offering customer service, supporting future activities, having input on future goods, and communicating, interacting, and sharing with consumers (valuable market insight!). Use the about area of the app to clarify how the system functions, and to direct the discussion and interaction that you want to see.

Track your progress

Using Facebook Insights (click "Insights" at the top of your page) to monitor your Facebook page's day-to-day success over a longer time. The Likes tab shows the total page development, and when the community views you. In contrast, the Scope, Clicks, and Post tabs show you the styles of notification-text, links, photo, etc. are favored by your followers (for more comprehensive interaction details, click on individual posts), and when they are more likely to consume your behavior on Facebook.

Paid Advertising Strategy on Facebook

When making the marketing plan, a budget for Facebook ads is important as the demand for eyeballs on the platform's content is that all the time, in parallel with the platform, intentionally reducing organic (non-paid) scope-particularly for self-promotional Page posts. Facebook also intentionally restricts the inclusion in the material of the News Feed of Page Post and only includes sales messages-telling users to purchase items, inviting them to join a sweepstake, etc., and allows paid advertising much more important.

You wouldn't open a real-world company and only allow customers to show up and hold their attention. Where their interest is going without marketing, so a Facebook page is no different, thankfully, you don't need to pay: Facebook advertising can be a quick and successful way to draw potential followers, hold current fans interested, guide users to your page or encourage them to do anything they want on the road to meet their marketing goals.

Note and Consider this: When you devote only $1 a day in campaign expenditure on Facebook advertising, the material would be revealed to many thousand users who may not have seen it otherwise. When you do that, when your rivals aren't, you would be far ahead with your market position in the knowledge process.

The effectiveness of Facebook advertising is the boosting of posts
Update to rank. Boosted articles last three days and should increase the web scope for the users who see it organically. Boosted posts produce a collection of instant Facebook advertisements in general language, without any of the extensive editing choices provided via the primary Facebook advertising app. Boosted articles do as follows:

1. Create a sponsored write-ups ad within Digital Devices, and Web News Feeds for a Supported Content Ad.

2. Promote your post from followers, their families, and across a small range of variants like age, gender, interests, and position inside the smart devices and desktop Newsfeeds.

3. Promote Followers, or supporters 'News Feeds inside your smart devices such as mobile and desktop and web post.

The actual expense of an enhanced post relies on how many users Facebook chooses to want to connect to the specific piece of material.

Twitter Tips: Make Your Tweets get to the Top

Millions of companies, businesses, firms, organizations, and individuals utilize Twitter as a means of tracking their company interactions, communicating with clients, handling customer care problems, advertising deals, posting vibrant and entertaining material such as photos and videos, etc. all inside 140 characters a message.

Setup Strategy for Twitter Profile

Without a profile designed to knock the socks off your clients, no stellar Twitter plan is complete, so let's get started with some critical setup and optimizing some tips.

Twitter Top username, and a tip for the "Name" box

The username for Twitter is important because it will be part of your Twitter profile URL-the address you would use in all your publicity content to attract users to follow you on the social network.

Attempt to make your username easy, memorable, and quick. Many businesses use their company or brand name as their username to interpret as their URL. Unlike several other pages, Twitter will encourage you to use its Settings menu to adjust your username as many times as you like. Even, it is worth noting that if you've promoted a username for a bit, it won't make good business sense to turn to a different one randomly.

Note: If Twitter says 'Type your real name, and people will remember you,' this isn't the most potent corporate strategy. Enter your brand or company name here, as it will show in large, bold letters right at the top of your Twitter profile.

Write an engaging Twitter Bio, using real names

Your Profile on Twitter is expected to show up high in your personal or company name's site search results, and you will use the 160 characters organic correctly (the bio text is used as the summary of the search link and, of course, shows on your Twitter profile). Use the limited space to inform others who you are objectively and succinctly, what you are doing and why they should follow you; use an upbeat sound to represent the enjoyable and conversational nature of Twitter.

As a business owner, it's a smart idea to have the actual name of the individual who handles your Twitter page, so that people feel more comfortable talking to a human than a faceless logo. If you have space, you may also or even want to put in a URL, or @mentions to connect to certain accounts you are affiliated with, and hashtags relevant to the company or business, too - but be careful that it also does not screw up the readability and consistency of the bio as a whole.

Uploading a compelling Twitter profile image

Ditch the generic Twitter icon and choose your picture or company logo. You might also mix the two. Just make sure you see a name. Essentially, the one-to-one connections in Twitter imply that users can associate with a profile that shows a person's happy face far more than the dreaded default egg icon or something equally anonymous. Twitter recommends posting the profile picture at 400 x 400 pixels. Select or Click on the Edit profile button on your page to make an update to your header image, and then "Adjust your profile picture."

Twitter Content Strategy and Marketing

Is that twitter marketing strategy and process looking good? Awesome! Now let take a look at some content tactics to assist your brand appearance on Twitter attracts people's attention.

Using past success to shape future content and Sharing engaging content

To assist, build your followers, and develop relationships with buyers, give samples of the type of soap products you are producing, and all the benefits of each.

Using hashtags to link tweets, searches and drive engagement

Use # Hashtags to link the same kind of tweets and highlight your post. Top-trending hashtags display on the site of Facebook, which can be quickly identified via Twitter searches. This has been shown that tweets that contain hashtags earn twice as much attention than those missing them, and their use is important. You shouldn't add more than 3 to 5 hashtags per message, because it can get overwhelming for followers; engaging with tweets that contain more than two hashtag tails off significantly.

Pin valuable Twitter posts, use as a marketing opportunity

If you wish to emphasize a particular tweet, pin it to the top of your page, and corresponding tweets should appear below it for further viewing.

You can use the Twitter widget and Tweet button to Promote and sell
Twitter has its version of the Like Facebook tab, displaying a live preview of the recent activity in your Twitter feed, along with a Follow button and a tweet tab for users.

Using images from your soap products to boost interaction, as a substitute for text, and tease. Facebook video ads-brief bursts and live broadcasting of the soap goods via Periscope. Upload and tag several images to improve interaction.

Accept orders via Twitter: Why not use Twitter to take orders or bookings? When you want to give it a try but are afraid that it would crowd your main page, you can build a new Twitter account almost as quickly as you can commit it to order.

Paid Advertisement on Twitter

Although Twitter advertisement may not have the same incredible breadth as Facebook's resources, helping you meet a broader audience with your tweets may also be a persuasive tactic.

Pinterest tips: the way to marketing excellence

Pinterest encourages everyone to build and arrange virtual pinboards on almost any subject, then share such pins (which are most generally images but may also be in video form) with other Pinterest users and through websites, forums, and other social networks around the Web. It is also an ideal place to get lots of profits and sell soap products. You can sign up for a business account, or you can even turn your interest to a business account.

Ensure your username contains your product name as (soap business) Using the 'About' section to your benefit, and the summary you write in the About Pinterest section appears at the top of your profile page and serves to explain your brand and what you're doing.

Upload a high-profile image

The two most common styles of Pinterest brand profile photos are the logo of your business or if you are the figurehead of your firm, a picture of your head and shoulders-smiling, and happy, of course. Pinterest profile images pop up on the profile page inside a rectangular square and in circles next to shared links and reviews. Attach the website and check for trust.

Be consistent and original: Pin consistently and frequently a couple times a day is a decent goal-but keep the stream running steadily, without getting interrupted by massive bursts of activities when you haven't touched or posted on it for weeks. This technique will increase your publicity and avoid flooding your followers.

Run an offer on Pinterest

People always love having everything to sell with the term 'free,' 'discount,' or 'giveaway' in it - and Pinterest's visual design is a perfect way to have them noticed. You Can pin photos from your website and add a summary of the deal offered there.

Advertising on Pinterest By Promoted Pins

Promoted pins are a means to extend the organic scope of pins you like to attract more of your following. They appear in daily search results and feeds for categories, and are labeled with the name "Promoted Button." You just pay for the original "boost" when you pay to advertise an icon. All further contact or traffic created by feedback or re-pins (even after the promotion ends) is free. If handled correctly, it can be a cost-effective way to sell your content and drive your soap business objectives.

LinkedIn Tips: Network Like Clockwork

LinkedIn is the digital center of the internet for professionals and companies to link to the internet and promote their brand, experience, and skills. As a user on LinkedIn, you can use the website to create a professional profile and monitor one of the top search results for your name, develop an extensive network for your soap company, among other items. Although you need to arrange your profile and company website before things can work properly, that involves a strong product profile, a soap business logo, and photos of the soap banners. Those have to be created professionally. It will help in the marketing of your soap business.

To create a strong business partnership, you'll need to pursue the like-mind client. Also, the community of soap similar to each other and be constructive to highlight your soap company.

YouTube Tips: Video Made the Marketing Star

Amid increasing pressure from Facebook and other smaller rivals, YouTube remains the most successful online video production and distribution site in the world. As a marketing medium, it is utterly brilliant.

Using the power of video in conjunction with other social networking platforms to show off your company to the world has many advantages, and you can enjoy the benefits of YouTube for good. You need to build a strong profile with the highest quality description; not all of that, you need to establish a sequence of your soap products with a show in the minds of buyers/customers to Youtube audiences, make your soap products stand out. Fill in your keywords on the list, and link your soap website with your YouTube channel for publicity. Set up a video ad on Fan Finder for free channel access. You should apply a watermark (soap) label to your videos.

If you have opened a YouTube account and released your first video, seek to upload videos regularly and frequently, not just abandon your account afterward.

Write effective video descriptions

Ensure your video description statements show in YouTube search results with the same few lines of it also appear below your video page text, accompanied by a "See More" button. Also, never neglect to tag your video the connection that has to be clicked on to read the rest.

Create custom video thumbnails (soap making goods or soap making business) all the way around. Through the show, you can create your soap business and invite viewers to watch and record demonstrations and feedback on the product. Advertise your latest soap products whenever you produce one.

Paid Advertising on YouTube

YouTube is one of just a couple of channels with more than a billion active monthly visitors with more viewers watching every day. It makes sense to start working with paying advertisements on the web, for such a large and varied audience.

Instagram Tips: Snap-happy Marketing Strategy

Millions of people use Instagram as a means of turning daily images and videos into memory-laden content with filters and frames, that can be shared with the world. The prospects are that your brand's (soap production) photos and videos are already on Instagram, and all of this content serves as genuine peer-to-peer endorsements of you, mainly free advertising. These guidelines are related to Facebook and Twitter for knowing and utilizing Instagram. So, just go over, read, and then apply it.

PART TWO: CANDLE MAKING BUSINESS

CHAPTER 8

THE HISTORY AND LANGUAGE OF CANDLES

The History of Candlemaking

The Candle occupies a distinct place in the history of man. True, many people still see candles as something that can only be used on holidays like Christmas or just for special dinner parties, but more and more of us find that we enjoy candles every day. While the exact origin and single inventor of the Candle is hard to pin down, we do know an incredible amount about the Candle. Humble as they may seem, candles from Roman Italy to the Qin Dynasty of ancient China have a long and storied history. Over thousands of years, society has depended on candles, and many great people around the globe have contributed to the creating and development of candles as we know them today.

The Earliest Traces of Candlelight

The use of candles and its improvements in the manufacture of candles have a parallel human journey back from the Stone Age. The

Egyptians used wicked candles as early as 3000 BC, where the first wicked candles are attributed to the early Romans. The Romans dipped wrapped papyrus into molten beeswax or tallow. Then, the resulting candles were used to light up their houses.

However, references to candles and Candles have been used for more than 5,000 years. Candles are a simple concept. Candles were produced in several different countries across the globe, separately. For several specific purposes and times, they have been used. They have traditionally provided a critical source of illumination for households and enterprises, and have also been commonly used in religious and spiritual worship. Given the invention of the electronic light bulb, the Candle has never failed or stopped to fascinate human beings. Perhaps this is because a candle generates both fire and light, and the fire created is essential to human existence.

A light bulb is a spark attempting to burn in a vacuum, after all. But a candle offers the real thing: you can see the fire, you can feel the heat, the smell of the aromas.

My sense of interest in the use of candles, both commercially available and more, being made both by the professional handcrafters and the ordinary home candlemakers, is that it is a reaction against the alienating experience of anything technological. Ancient candles were produced using tallow wax, which was extracted from sheep, cow meat, and unwinded twine threads, according to studies. The custom of creating candles using molds started in France in the fifteenth century. The wax was squeezed into open, ended hollow tubes. Such cylinders had a cap in the middle for wicking with a tiny tube.

The wick was then put in the pot, and short wires left in place. The candles were pulled tightly until the mold had been full, and the wax allowed to cool.

Colonial women gave America's first approach to the production of candles as they have learned boiling grayish-green berries from the bay-berry shrub, they could produce a lovely wax. This wax has developed an attractive fragrance and a perfect burning candle. The method of removing or extracting the wax from the bayberries was, however, extremely tedious and tired. A few fifteen pounds of boiled bayberries will offer only one pound of wax.

The candle industry today offers candle lovers a broad variety of candles made from slightly different waxes. Such candles are sold in a broad variety of colors, forms, patterns, and fragrances. Candles can no longer be the sole source of illumination, but they symbolize holidays, mark affection, soothe the senses, describe rituals, and accent homes across the world. Nowadays, candles are mainly used as decoration or as a means to infuse of fragrance.

What is candle making business?

Do you ever question yourself often saying, (is candle making a successful business to embark on?)

The information which makes a candle a good decision for business

Candles are used by 70percent out of households in U.S. Depending on your targeted market, you can sell candles from $5US, and up anywhere. In high-end markets, Candles can be sold according to your imaging profit. Candles are sold at over $4 billion per annum.

Step 1: Learn The Candle Making Technique

Candlemaking is a talent crafting. It comprises of natural and synthetic ingredients, various scents, varying the amount of perfume to please the consumer, incorporating color and texture, and also creating the wax with specific designs, overlays, or paint variations. Candle making is a crafting and can be very exciting business.

You may want to do your due diligence before offering your homemade product if you find candle making looks very simple. You need to create and settle on candles:

1. What wax you will be working with palm wax, soy, beeswax or paraffin.
2. The color quantity and variations you'll have (tie-die, designs, layering, etc.).

3. Scents you will work with or the containers you'll use it's shapes.

Step 2: Stabilize your Cost and Quality

You might be able to begin your business at home, using your kitchen heat source and utensils, while depending on local zoning laws. Many places, like Candle Science and Candle hem, will purchase a tool package for the starters online. Your candle materials shouldn't cost more than a few hundred dollars, to begin with.

These includes:

- Paraffin, beeswax, gel, soy, and some wax
- Packaging supplies
- Wicks
- Essential oils are needed for fragrance or aroma.
- Jars, tins or other containers
- Coloring agents
- Shipping costs of raw materials or products in and finished products out.

Many start-up expenses may require software creation, which, depending on the area expertise, will cost nil to a couple of hundred dollars and at least a relatively decent video.

You will always be referring to an insurance provider in the first instance. Because there is the risk for fire incidents, you ought to be sure that the operation is fire-insured so that you have a fire extinguisher at the premises. In addition, you can have an introductory interview with a prosecutor to determine what the relevant license or authorization criteria are.

The major expenses in a candle making business

The market mainly revolves around the various kinds of wax, the pots, and ingredients to paint and scent. After you have started small and shown that your business plan can succeed, you will buy these goods in bulk at a reduced cost per package.

Step 3: Begin Building Your 7 Business Systems

The business systems including:

1. The Lead Generation System

Your Consumer Intake Method is the lead generation device. Using ads, advertisements, public relations, and outbound sales, the lead generation program attracts outsiders to your company.

These are some things you'll need to do to get your lead system generation running is:

- Setting up Your Website
- Sign up for Craft Fairs, local stores, Farmers Markets
- Get referrals from family and friends
- Give Some Away as Gifts so that More People can experience and give feedback on your product

- Use Search Engine Optimization (SEO) on Online Listings and Your Website.
- Set aside some budget for paid advertising

2. Lead Conversion System

You would have to find a way to turn a lead into a consumer because the traffic is flowing to you from the lead generation Program. You can have a long or short funnel that does the job or work. Many bloggers, for example, have cold traffic (people who don't recognize their brand) going to their websites. They have to create confidence from there, and customers sign up for their mailing list, so they will not purchase or buy for years.

You may have a long or short time, depending on the lead conversion method, to convert a lead into a conversion. A short funnel can build confidence quickly: live networking, useful contributions, or even webinars will aid.

Below are more things you can do to boost up your lead conversional system:

- Setup up a Shopping Cart on your Website.
- Consider setting up or creating accounts with Distribution Partners like Amazon, FBA, or Etsy.
- Master outbound sales for the times when you're live networking.

- Create a Contact Us page and a FAQ page, so that customers can get questions about your product been answered

3. Branding System

Whether your lead generation method or your branding program usually is the first experience to your clients, and when you grow them, you'll want to remember that. The company has the mark and paint selection, but it's a lot more than that; it's your customer's perception about you.

For what you will charge for goods or services, the name will make a big impact, and you want to build something that creates value. What you do is 50% of your brand. What the customer perceives or percepts as a result of what you do is the other 50%. Therefore, you'll need or wants to take lots of initiative and creativity in your brand management.

Here are some things to put on your branding system.

- Create or make a logo
- Choose a niche
- Develop your color palette and fonts
- Write your mission, purpose, vision, and dream
- Create your pitch of elevator
- How you'll build reputation and trust with customers
- Get clear about your "Why."

4. Client Fulfillment System

Stabilizing the expenses and mastering the methodology all fall under consumer service. However, some other components to consider are:

- Creating a schedule and budget for your business
- Mapping your customer journey and identifying pain points
- How you'll get feedback and testimonials
- How you'll ensure quality
- Money-back guarantees and alleviating customer risk
- How to make money from candle making business?

Candlemaking firms offer candles either directly to customers or indirectly by resellers, such as boutiques, gift shops, and other shopping outlets for the arts and crafts. Candlemaking is a very general area, so establish distinction by the types of candles you sell (pillar, floating, votive, tea, etc.), or by the price of the bid. Experiment with colors, scents, and molds to create something worthy of premium pricing with a unique appeal.

Furthermore, Often, search for sources of raw materials at the lowest possible prices, with optimum profit margins on your profits. Include similar items or candle styles to broaden the target market too.

5. Job Prototypes

If you intend to get support, you want to be specific on will role's limits, so everybody understands their priority, and things run smoothly. As an aid, it may get challenging as the organizational process and tasks become ambiguous. Similarly, whether the client refuses to be turned off or is unsure who can go to for what, it may be off-putting and even lead them to leave.

Until you get in front of people (especially in a live setting), you want to build job prototypes where you separate the tasks required to operate the company and remind any helper of the tasks they are in control of and for which they are going to be a backup.

6. Management System

Someone will track the procedures, create training manuals, ensure that people stick to their work templates, and record discrepancies between training manuals and template and actual life. Such managers are part of the Management structure.

They help you keep the company engine going reliably well and ideally grow stronger over time. Their input would cause changes to be made to the training guides and work designs to make them more reliable or to improve rate of turnover.

How much can you charge customers?

Candle products may sell for as little as a couple of bucks or more as $20US. The consistency and scope of your product portfolio, your marketplace, marketing plan, and competitiveness would rely on your pricing. If your goal is to be the lowest vendor, make sure that you get your raw materials at really good prices, and that you know what your rivals demand. You will possibly want to purchase wicks, wax, coloring agents, scents, and other bulk materials to get full savings per product.

If the aim is to sell a rather premium line of goods, the cost is less of a problem as long as the items are aesthetically outstanding. When you want a supermarket reseller that will move a ton of your products, you might always want to give significant discounts on prices.

How much profit can you earn in a candle-making business?

This is possible to make a net profit of 50 percent or more. Materials costs aren't much high, so be sure you can completely invest the resources required to make your candle business successful.

The best ways to increase the profitability of your Candle business?

When you become an expert at the fundamentals of making candles, try expanding out with the kinds of products you sell. For example, studying how to mold or carve candles to any form will boost profit and benefit potential. And, using liquid candles to continue selling sophisticated oil lamps. You could learn how to create these adds to the may product line in certain situations, or figure out where to purchase them for resale.

When you have a studio with the space required, consider offering classes on candle making. You may contact your local community center or community college to see if they might be interested in introducing your course to their program in this initiative.

The Nineteen Century Candle Making

During the 19th century, the manufacturing of candles began to become a big industry. They designed and patented candle making machines. With mass production in full operation, the majority of households could afford candles.

During this time, the braided wicks still used today were invented, and a breakthrough in candle-making took place. The animal fats which were previously used in candles making contain stearic acid, which was discovered by two chemists. They later patented a method for making candles using crude stearic acid, which improved the quality of candles significantly.

The Twenty-century candle making

In the beginning of the 20th century, candles gained increased success as the rise of the U.S. oil and meat processing industries caused an improvement in byproducts that had been the essential ingredients of candles, which is paraffin and stearic acid.

Candle popularity stayed steady until later when interest in candles as decorative items, mood-setters, and gifts began to rise significantly. Soon candles became available in a broad variety of styles, shapes, and colors, and consumer desire in scented candles started to rise.

Nowadays Candles

Even though candles are no longer used as a major light source, they continue to increase in popularity and usage. Candles are used today to symbolize a party, spark passion, soothe the senses, celebrate service, and highlight home decors cast a moist and lovely light for all to appreciate.

Candle-making is now an art form nowadays. Many companies concentrate on making wonderful candles with a range of exclusive fragrances. Many local companies also concentrate on producing home-cooking candles. Candle making today is more than just a business; it can also be a great hobby and an enjoyable activity for the whole family.

Candles are often used as comfort and enjoyment, instead of using candles for light and heat. When the candle business expands, it produces different styles of candles. The range of colors, fragrances, and candle styles to pick from is incredible.

The candles are a very common home decoration choice. They can be used to accentuate any place. Sometimes, for dinners or other formal events, they deliver an outstanding centerpiece. There is a strong sense of heritage in American culture in the peace candles which are used at weddings.

Candle making is an art style that has evolved radically over the years. It is a pretty simple method if you're involved in wanting to make your own. To get used to the making phase, it is best to start with a container candle or a votive. You will find a broad variety of Candle making kits at a low price or books that can give you advice and support in the process.

CHAPTER 9

MISTAKES TO AVOID WHEN BEGINNING A CANDLE-MAKING BUSINESS

A candle-making company is one choice among many when you plan to establish your own work-at-home business. Starting a home business with a candle can be enjoyable and entertaining, and a way to make use of your creativity. Before you begin, though, there are several items to think about that will help secure your business success. Avoid errors that could cause the business to go bankrupt before it even begins.

Mistake 1 - Starting without Experience

You must have at least some experience before you start, just as with any home business. You have a head start on developing a company if you've made candles as a hobby or for informal gift-giving. It would take more time to establish every business with little expertise, and it poses more risk. Only attending a workshop at a nearby community center or reading a candle-making book will give you any startup background.

Mistake 2 - not having a Market

Deciding when and how you should market your candle until you are official in your company is essential. The easiest way to sell the goods is to get a website, although there are other ways too.

No matter whether you market the candles, you'll need to be sure that the quality is correct, and you can attract and retain a client base and eventually generate a profit for yourself. Avoiding errors and getting fun can drive you deep into the business of producing candles.

Mistake 3 - Not having a Research and Business Plan

A good marketing plan is a must, and much work goes hand-in-hand with that. Creating candles as a hobby or for fun is a straightforward start; it takes some preparation to move them to a business stage. You may need to explore where to buy bulk materials, including molds, candle base (whether beeswax, paraffin, gel, or soy), wicks, dyes, and oils that are scented. On the practical hand, when picking a company name and registering the company in the local city or state, you may need to prepare for the business. You'll still need a business license in some instances, even though you operate a business from your house.

Mistake 4 - not having a Niche

Settling on the production of candles as a commercial enterprise requires choosing a niche. If you enjoy creating a certain kind of candle and are efficient in producing it, that should be your priority.

For starters, if you've made soy candles, continue with making soy candles until you're ready to expand your business, or until there's a significant financial justification for making other types of candles. The possibilities are various and broad, including floating, votives, mixed colors, unique occasions, and as well as various scented.

Mistake 5 - not having a Work Space

When you want to set up a business from home, you need to make sure that you have the necessary room to support your business. You needed space to melt your candle material with a candle making service, whatever it's that you want. You need a place to store the components of your candle; molds, pot melting, wicks, and oils, etc. You will need to be prepared to store everything you produce and to do bookkeeping and selling research in office space. Structured workspace tends to make you more effective and productive.

The Diffcrent Types Of Candles

Container candles

Candles are poured into a sort of jar that holds the molten wax when it melts. Typically, such candles are produced from soft wax.

Pillar candles

Thick wax columns which can be made in a number of geometrical shapes.

They are unevenly shaped candles that are produced in the style of different objects/figurines by molding or sculpting wax.

Tapers

Tall, slim candles around 1/2-1 inch in diameter and ideal for fitting in a candle holder. This is the usual dinner table candles and is created by dipping the wick regularly into a wax jar before the taper is of the exact diameter. Tapers may also be made by molding or by wrapping wax sheets around a wick.

Votives

Thick, tiny candles about 2 inches in diameter and 2-3 inches height. They are usually used for scent in little spaces such as the toilets.

Tea lights

Small containers candles that are used for warming Pourri pots and food trays.

Ways of candle making

Molding

Candles are created by pouring wax into molds. Candle molds can be sold in hobby stores/candle supplies, or you can make the molds out of cartons, boxes, plastic forms, etc. You may also create your molds using a rubber mold pack.

Dipping

Tapers are simply produced by repeated dipping a wick's length into a molten wax bath. Hardens each sheet, rendering the taper deeper and deeper. A tapered design produces the inherent influence of gravity. A pair of tapers are typically created to ensure that the thickness fits. This is achieved by keeping a double wick length in the middle and dipping both sides, such that two tapers are formed at the same time.

Poured

Poured candles pertain to any candle created by pouring wax into a molded form, including container candles, cast candles, and molded candles.

Rolled

Most rolled candles are the simplest to produce, probably. They're made by spinning wax sheets around the wick. This process may be used to create tapers, bases, and novelty candles.

Why you should Make Your Candles?

If you're still pondering about giving a candle, having a shot or not, then reading through the list below may help you take a decision.

Making candles may be an operation of profit and fulfillment. Candles are lovely to have on hand for a number of occasions, making them flexible and functional home decor pieces, let alone valuable resources in case of an electrical outage. Candle-making can be enjoyable and entertaining, so there are many advantages to this until you know the technique and do so.

1. You Can widen your creativity!

With each passing year, the effects of fun aromatic environments are more apparent. It is not aromatherapy but candle therapy, a blend of two senses to establish an unrivaled feeling of well-being and absolute joy.

Creating your candles is easy; it takes very little time; it uses only products you already have at home so that it will have the environmental effect (in terms of packaging so transport costs). Ultimately, you have an element that is you in terms of scents and colors, beautifully matching with your house. They should not ignore the benefits of distinct scents. In the end, you have an item, which is wholly you in terms of aromas and colors, blending perfectly with your home. We should not overlook the benefits of distinctive aromas. You'll find one that renders relaxation almost compulsive, another one that follows fine dining and pictures the fire that invites your partner home to the hope of a passionate night?

You may render your candles as plain or complicated as you like them to be. There is no doubt about what you can and can't do for candles created by yourself. Indeed, some of your concepts might not be as well as you might have liked, but they help you to know and develop with the next ones!

The numerous methods which are out there when it comes to producing different styles of candles are infinite and are still that and improving to this day.

2. Make Money

Not only that, you will save money, but by producing your candles, you can earn money too. Establishing a home-based candle company will help you boost your earnings when doing something you enjoy. If a business seems too large and complex, at fairs and community events, you can start by hosting a candle-stall. You may launch an online store running from your own home without having any extra room or money. Scented candles, design candles, and specially formed candles are only some of the suggestions that the crowds will bring in. Candles are used during the year, and persistent demand for handcrafted candles will be present.

3. Know Precisely What Ingredients Are Going Into Your Candlemaking

With the increasingly growing issues about using environmentally sustainable and safe materials in products around us, make the candles an even better choice. Some of the candle makers have adjusted to the evolving times and use certain additives more often today, but you will never say with certainty until you try it yourself.

4. Creating Your Scent Combinations or Choosing Your Fragrances

This point can go hand and hand with the previous one, but I believe it merits it spot on the list.

Two people will not have similar likes when it comes to the smell of a candle. The strength of the fragrances is also one of the reasons that can trigger the most important differences of opinion among all lovers of candles. Many people enjoy candles that are so strong they can spread the scent around a whole space just before they're even lit, while others like it when you can only get faint traces of scent here and there.

Candle manufacturers are unable to satisfy the needs of all, and so producing their candles is a perfect opportunity for experimentation. Do you have a smell you would like to go after? Think of the primary ingredients that produce it, and check variations of scent oils to build it.

5. They are simple to make and fun!

It is as easy as restocking and getting one of the products you just finished using! You will seem like a professional in no time.

6. Save Money

Making handmade candles is a perfect way to save money. You not only won't need to purchase the candles, but you will still save money on friends and family presents. Buying bulk supplies would help you save money on the raw materials you require for this project.

CHAPTER 10

HOW TO GET STARTED IN CANDLE MAKING

Candle making has developed from the requisite work into an art performed by imaginative people who love learning new skills. If you master these important skills, which are outlined in the following sections, you will be able to create candles in all types, sizes, and styles and let your creativity soar.

Candle Making Terminology

Before we start, let us review the several types of candles and some standard candle-making terms that you ought to know.

The National Candle Association has given the subsequent definitions.

Candle: A combustible wicks backed by a material that forms a fuel, which can be solid, quasi-rigid, or semi-solid at a temperature of 68–80° Fahrenheit. Candles can hold additives, which are used for durability, color, scent, or to adjust the burning features of the wax base. The merged purpose of these is to nurture a light-producing flame.

Candle Accessory: An object, i.e., a candle-holder or candle tray, created for use with a candle or candles.

Filled Candle: otherwise called a container candle, this is a candle produced and used in the same container, or vessel. Several containers can be reused and refilled.

Freestanding Candle: This term applies to a rigid candle in the form of an object (a pillar-shaped, column-shaped, or novelty candle).

Freestanding candles are safer when mounted on a non-flammable, heat-resistant base, such as a plate or metal tray, or a distinctive candle attachment designed for that purpose.

Taper Candle: A taper candle is a thin candle, generally 10-12 in height, designed to be held by a candle holder, normally a glass, crystal, or metal candlestick with a well in the middle that is similar with the diameter of the base of the candle. Bought taper candles to match standard candlesticks come in small sizes.

Tealight Candle: A spherical filled candle produced about 1.5 "(38 mm) and 0.75" (19 mm) in diameter and height, accordingly. Tealight candles are generally used to warm foods, but they can be used as small receptacles and candle shell fillers.

Votive Candle: A candle created for use in a candle case, typically a standard votive candleholder, a spherical (usually made of glass) vessel of the same scale as the votive candle. Votives may also be mounted like freestanding candles on a smooth, non-flammable sheet. They are fun to use to suit a specific design or seasonal style in groups of one color or many colors.

Votive Holder: A tiny transparent vessel to carry a votive candle as it burns. The votive holder must be in a spot to accommodate the molten candle wax.

Wax: This is a solid or semi-solid substance composed of a mixture of hydrocarbons and derivatives of hydrocarbons.

Wick: A string-like material that supplies fuel to a flame via the capillary or wicking action process.

Wax Candle: A candle having as its primary fuel: petroleum wax, food wax animal wax, or bug wax.

Equipment For Candle Making

Metal Pouring Jug

This jug is used to spill hot wax into pots and molds and is the best jar to keep molten wax when dipping candles. Since the pouring must be performed carefully and without splashing, it is suggested to get a jug made with a shaped spout. Select a model with a half-gallon of liquid in it. Pouring pot is an imperative piece of candle producing wax-melting equipment.

Digital scale

The correct quantities of paraffin ought to be measured. The best method for measuring candle-making materials is by weight, so the appropriate scale is needed. Measuring by volume isn't accurate or precise.

If you're working with limited quantities, measuring inaccuracies are stepped up. A more or less ounce of oil in a volume which has a cumulative weight of 12 pounds does not create a substantial difference. Even one ounce short or extra in a 1-pound combination is a major difference that can either make a substance more alkaline or oily.

You could splurge on several of your candle making supplies but bring the money on a respectable scale. It will repay you time and time again with trust, comfort, and peace of mind. It is advisable to cover the wireless scale under plastic wrap or in a plastic bag with zip closure so that the keypad is not harmed.

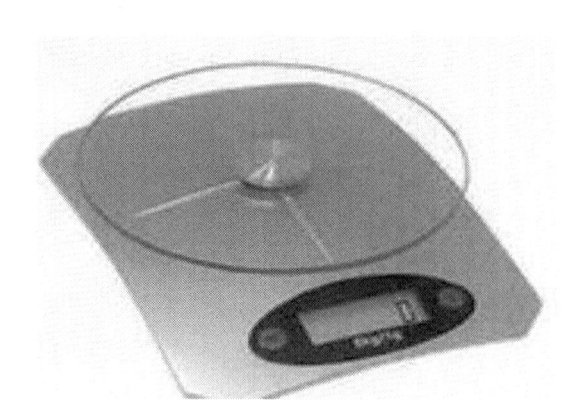

Thermometers

Your thermometer is important, albeit a tiny element in your array of candle-making devices. A unique wax thermometer may be obtained or chocolate or other cooking thermometer covering a scale from 0 to 300 °

Fahrenheit used. It will have a clip so you can dive it far enough into your melting wax pot to get a detailed interpretation.

Make sure the thermometer is correct — a thermometer of candy. You also have to ask the exact degree the wax has been heated to. Just a few degrees higher than the point of fire is a hazard. When it is no longer reliable, test the thermometer frequently, and discontinue the use.

A candy or food thermometer, varying from 100- to 356-degrees F. For the analysis of molten wax levels, between 38- and 180-degrees C. Expect paying about $20, which is available in most kitchen equipment shops, and design stores.

You'll want to pour out your single pour wax at 145-150, and your votive/mold wax at 160-165 for better performance.

As the pouring temperature is so vital, a thermometer is a must for candle making.

Candlewick has a regular thermometer for candles (M-61) and a modern top-end thermometer. Both are efficient at reading wax temperature.

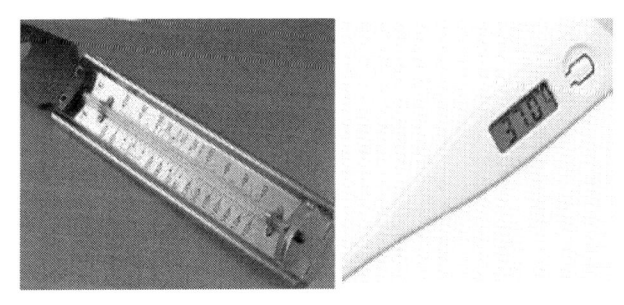

Wax

Paraffin, a petroleum by-product, is the preferred wax in this book for making the candle hot-wax designs. In certain art hardware shops, Candlewic stocks over 20 separate waxes of odorless, colorless, and fairly cheap, standard paraffin. Please remember that each variation of candle wax would have specific melting points, characteristics, and temperatures to pour. You will need container wax if you're putting wax in a jar or tin or pillar wax, which is a harder wax for candles that stand on their own.

Double Boiler

A 2-quarter size model made of stainless steel or aluminum is suggested for use with heat paraffin to facilitate cleanup. You may also make an unconventional double boiler by placing a tiny casserole within a larger one. Try utilizing old pots and pans for candle making purposes, as the wax is very difficult to extract completely from pans.

The double boilers are incredibly simple to improvise, as you can see. You do need an outer pot to carry water and an inner pot (insert) to drop the wax into. The outer pot must be reasonably wide to accommodate a sufficient volume of water to lift two-thirds of the way up the inner pot. Optimally the inner pot should have a handle (excellent for a metal pitcher).

A big bowl, like the type fruit juice that is sold in, would work if you're able to ladle the wax out. When you use mitts to shield your hands from fire, and you are very patient, you may pour from such a glass. Whatever sort of double-boiler you have, you may need to regularly refill the water in the bottom pot to hold your boiling water at the appropriate stage.

Heat Source

Perfect for heating candle wax to the correct temperature is an electric or gas stove.

An electronic hot plate, which is sold in most department or kitchen equipment shops, often works great as well.

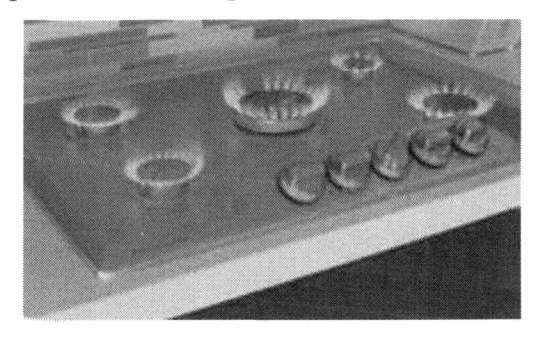

Wick

Wick scale needs to fit to accommodate the candle's diameter for optimal burning.

A wick so low can dissolve quickly in a tub of molten wax. Too large a wick can flame, sputter and burn too dry. Manufacturers use a labeling scheme that defines the right variations of wick/candle, so bear this in mind when shopping.

For optimal burning, the most regular-size candles, some up to 3 inches in diameter, need just one central wick. Big candles can require two wicks spaced equally or more.

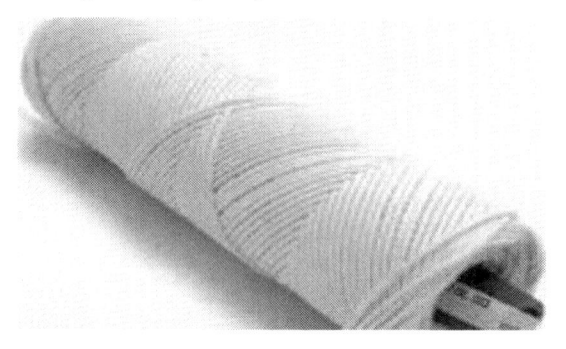

Wire Core

Cotton core and wire core are the two primary forms of the wick. Cotton core wick, which typically consists of "braided" threads around a dense cotton base, is preferred to create poured, dipped, and beeswax candles. This can be a circular braid or flat braid.

It is suggested that wire core wick be used in container candles, which burn the longest of all candles. As the name implies, a thin strip of metal, typically made of zinc passes along the middle of the wick, providing it more support and enabling it to flame higher than the normal wick for a longer time. Stop using older core wick wire, because it can contain lead, a common key element that was used in manufacturing years ago. The use was abandoned owing to health issues. Consumer wicks are fairly cheap and very durable, and it is not advised to use handmade wicks made of paper or twine.

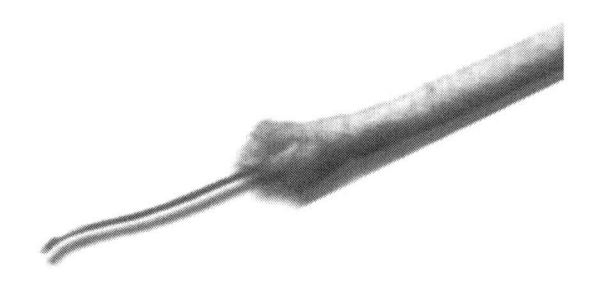

Stainless Steel Measuring Cups

Mold Sealer

To stop wax from leaking, this sticky gum-like substance plugs the wick hole at the bottom of a candle mold. It is often used to keep the wick tab within the bottle when poured hot wax.

Dye

Commercial candle dyes are focused on creating solid, dark colors around the color spectrum in a limited volume. The dye is provided in chips or rough squares. Normally between '8 and' 4 ounces of dye is adequate for 1 pound of paraffin to stain. Since dye formulations differ from manufacturer to manufacturer, you will obey the instructions from the packets.

Mixing dyes can be made from unique paints, just as artists do for their palettes. For example, applying yellow and blue dyes to wax would produce a green shade. Creating a common, personalized paint is a trial and error exercise.

Homemade dyes or other colors not explicitly intended for the manufacture of candles should be avoided because igniting them could prove dangerous, or they could clog the wick and keep it from burning properly. It can not be used for crayons for this same purpose.

Note: The proportions you combine into the wax will produce various shades of these colors.

Scent Disks Or Fragrance Oil

Like pigment dyes, oils and fragrances are potent — a little goes a long way. Oils are designed to mix well with melted wax, which, when burnt, offer off a heavy aroma; scented disks come in solid shape, just like dye disks, which are not typically as aromatic.

1/4 to 1/8 ounce of oil is appropriate for 1 pound of wax for most consumer perfume preparations. Commonly produced scents include chocolate, lavender, cinnamon, lilac, honeysuckle, rose, gardenia, strawberry, coconut, jasmine, hyacinth, patchouli, blueberry, bayberry, sandalwood, banana, orange, grapefruit, cherry, apple, peach, mulberry, tangerine, pine, patchouli, mint, coffee, vanilla, and clove. You can blend the scents to produce unique results.

Beeswax Sheets

Such textured, rectangular sheets are usually sold in packs of two, each around 8 inches wide and 18 inches tall, made from pressed and molded beeswax. The sheets are mildly oily and pliable and are ready to roll directly from the package.

There is no need to apply coloring or scent because the sheets are already prepared for usage. Candlewick is also included with the package; make sure to review the contents.

Containers

Glass canning or jelly jars are best suited for creating candles, as they are built without cracking to withstand high temperatures. Steel containers and ceramic mugs, as long as they may endure intense flame and fire, can also be used.

Most art shops sell a range of simple and decorative glass jars for crafts with candles.

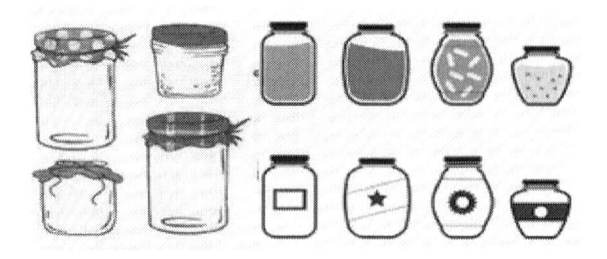

Candle Molds

They are typically made from rigid plastic, brass, iron, or rubber and come in various shapes and lengths.

For the projects detailed in this book, a durable plastic pillar mold is suggested simply to manage, easy to clean-that holds a pound of wax. Many plastic molds, such as rectangles, triangles, and pyramids, may be used to create candles in geometric ways.

Scissors Or Craft Knife

Once the candle has cooled, each should perform perfectly to cut the wick to the correct length and trim it. Cutting beeswax sheets before rolling requires a craft knife.

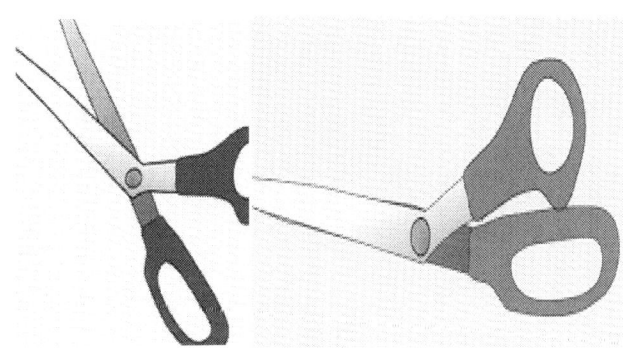

Apron

This defends clothes from irregular wax drips and spills. Even if you don't require absolute overalls, you do at least require protective goggles, protective gloves, and an apron. They cover your eyes, hands, and clothing from any unintended caustic splashes.

Oven Mitts

Any mitts built for kitchen usage would fit great before and after the pouring of molten wax to treat hot pans, molds, and containers.

Spoon

Get a spoon about 12 inches long with a handle, so you can comfortably mix dyes and scent oils into the wax.

Wooden Ice Cream Sticks

They represent two purposes in the production of candles. The stick protects the wick to prevent it from slipping into the mold or bottle during the pouring of hot wax.

This is often used to poke holes in the cooling wax coating such that the trapped air is released.

Cutting Board Or Placemat

This gives a flat, untextured surface for beeswax candles to roll. It is Recommended here to have a glass or plastic top.

Measuring Spoons

For applying stearin and fragrances to the hot wax, a set of metal or plastic, measuring spoons comprising regular measures (teaspoons/tablespoons) is recommended.

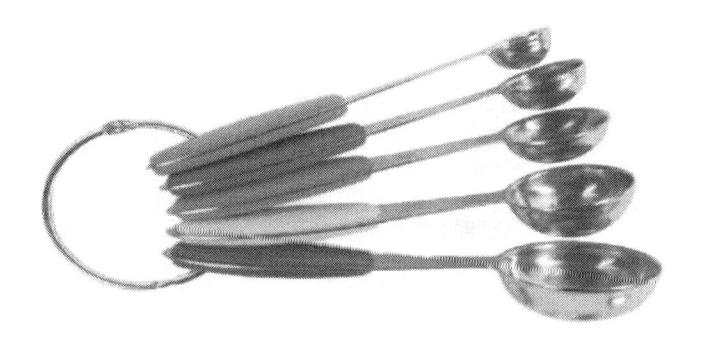

Ruler Or Straight-Edge

It is used as a guide when you are cutting beeswax sheets.

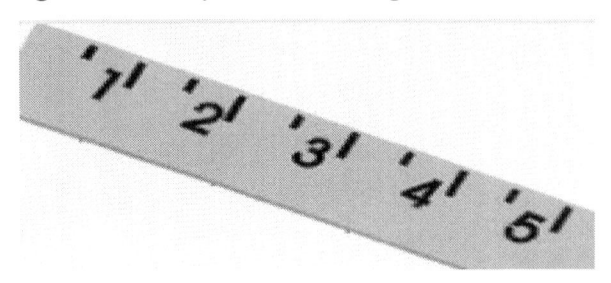

Hair Dryer

They are used to heat cold sheets of beeswax to make them lighter and more convenient to roll.

Newspapers

Old newsprint should avoid the wax drips and drops from your countertops and other areas of your workspace—sufficient secure papers to protect three to four sheets of surfaces at the job area.

Paper Towels, Cleaning Rag

Hold any on hand at the end of the project for the fast removal of drips and spills and cleaning equipment.

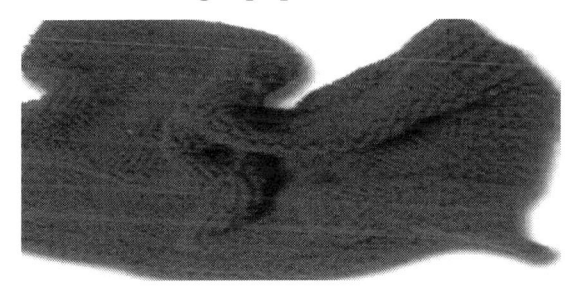

Wax Paper

When you are rolling freshly dipped candles to smooth them out, the non-stick properties of wax paper are needed. The paper may also be used for producing rolled beeswax candles to cover work surfaces; a flat cutting board or laminated placemat works great for beeswax candles too.

Empty Coffee Can

It is used to hold leftover wax for projects yet to come.

Small Plastic Bags

The form used for sandwiches is ideal for holding supplies of candles such as dyes and wick stock.

Nylon Stocking

Imperfections on a candle's surface can be buffed off with a strip of pantyhose nylon. Use an old item, as it is hard to strip the wax from the material.

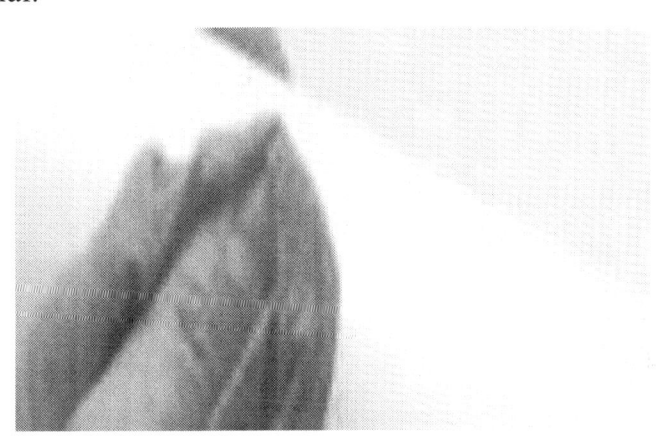

A Good Working Area

The ordinary kitchen offers the appropriate workspace to produce pots, shaped and dipped candles, providing the region where hot wax is poured within easy reach of a heat source.

Any solid, flat surface will do for the rolled beeswax idea, which doesn't require melting wax.

Clear away from countertops near the work area, small appliances, utensil holders, and other products. Despite care and diligence throughout the creation of candles, any hot wax appears to often make its way to areas not coated with newspaper. A little energy expended shifting these little things can now save time when it comes to later cleaning. For projects involving melting wax, a handy supply of water-be it from a faucet or container such as a broad pitcher-is required. It is a good idea to have a clock nearby to gage time in the projects as necessary.

In the absence of a kitchen, a workspace can be created in an environment such as the basement or garage. Projects involving melted wax require a portable hot electric plate and counter/table system. Ensure an electrical socket is available from the workroom, so the table is wide enough to fit both supplies and equipment.

Making candles demands your concentration in full, without interruption. If, at the outset of will process, you do not have the sum of time stated, consider postponing the session until the period permits.

Candle making Safety Or Precaution

If you have never produced candles before, you could not be sure of the steps that you need to take to prevent accidents or damage. Many chemicals used in the manufacturing of candles may be dangerous if not correctly handled, so here are a few health tips to keep you healthy when producing candles.

Each moment you operate with an open flame, all the elements for a potentially unsafe scenario are there. You must be conscious and strictly adhere to safety guide. The creation of candles needs your in-divisive focus. Talk not even about multitasking when dealing with hot wax.

Also, the decision comes down to personal desire though paraffin wax is the cheapest and easiest for the novice since it easily takes on aromas and colors.

Beeswax is easier to mix but has its own distinctive and delicate flavor. However, you use to break the wax into small parts, shavings perform very well because this facilitates a smooth melting process and prevents visible temperature variations. You could not leave that unattended at any point during the melting cycle. Mind that the wax is flammable then it wouldn't make a good candle

Spreading a newspaper, many sheets wide, in the field where you're employed is an ideal idea. The procedures for specific recipes are laid out below, but the last four phases, i.e., all melting and blending are finished, are the same in any situation.

Taking your preference mold cut a wick length approximately two inches extra and would be the same diameter as the candle. Wrap a pencil (or similar) across the end of the cut wick long enough to fit around the mold. Enable wick to trail to the bottom of your mold.

Gently pour the molten wax mixture into the container, which should be put on a flat surface and firmly left in position to prevent spillage, removing the wick and its holder. Put aside so it can cool off and solidify. It should require at least 16 hours to finish and is better kept 24 hours.

Softly unwind the wick holder, and then cut a large wick to a quarter of an inch, implying a more substantial flame and a shorter existence for the candle.

Step 1 – Ensure that you are using the right equipment.

- Use only containers that are rated for making candles. Vendors have certified all of the glass containers to be suitable for candles making.

- Verify that you have a thermometer to check the wax temperature. When it is so hot, it might theoretically smash the glass into which you pour it, produce a lot of smoke that may trigger respiratory issues, or become a fire hazard.

- You'll always want to make sure the jar in which you heat the wax is safe to treat. The smooth aluminum pouring pots are built with a plastic handle that you can comfortably hold, even if loaded with hot wax, with your bare hand.

- When using a mold for your candles or tarts, make sure it's made of a substance that can handle the molten wax's strength. Both the pillar molds, votive molds, silicone molds, and clamshells are healthy to use for producing candles or tarts because they are constructed of heat-resistant products.

Note: The clamshells are safe to create tarts, although it is not advisable to pour the wax in them unless it is 150 ° F or colder.

Step 2 – Ensure that you are using the correct materials.

- Just use wax created for making candles. When you use wax not intended for a candle, it may trigger respiratory issues or pose a possible fire hazard. Most of the waxes we bring are non-toxic and healthy to use while producing candles.

- Ensure that you use the scent oils or essential oils that are made to create candles. Perfumes cannot be used safely; they may be a possible fire threat and would certainly not give you a successful fragrance fall. Many of the oils to the fragrance can irritate the skin. Rinse the region with a cool wash, and a tube of liquid soap to rinse it up if you have some oil on your hands. We have about 400 scent oils, all safe to use while making candles.

- Verify that you have the right size wick for your candles. If you're using a wick that's too large, it will produce a lot of soot that might cause respiratory difficulties. If the flame is too wide and too dry, it may be a fire threat too, so ensure that you (and your customers) know how to trim the wick when it burns. There have also been instances where the wick burned so bright that it induced cracking or fracturing of the glass bottle, just be sure to perform a check burn and be sure the candle is not burning too bright. Note: If you are selling the candles, you must have a notice or alert sticker at the bottom of the candle that describes how to light a candle properly.

Step 3 – Ensure that your workspace is safe and organized.

- Ensure sure you keep the candles in a clean, well-ventilated environment, and you don't inhale it because of the fragrant oils in the "fumes." When you are exposed to them for extended periods without adequate ventilation, too much exposure to these scent oils can induce dizziness, headaches, or breathing issues. When making candles in your oven, turn the vent hood on to keep the air flowing. If your workspace is not fitted with a vent hood, open a window or door to help move the breeze.

- You might want to ensure that you take measures to shield yourself from the hot wax. Wearing gloves, long trousers, or even an apron is advised to prevent the skin from being burned by any wax that may spill about while pouring or stirring.

- Create a designated place for lighting up your candles. When the wax sets, they can stay anywhere, undisturbed, for many hours. When the work environment is tidy and healthy, ensuring sure you, and the candles, are free from any damage would be far simpler.

Candle Wax Additives

Additives (like petrolatum, vybar, etc)

Additives, when mixed with waxes, will harden, opacify, mottle, and produce other special effects. Normally, they can be melted with a limited quantity of the wax mix and applied to the remainder of the wax pan. This should guarantee melting properly and a comprehensive mixing.

Many additives will help differentiate your candles from your rivals, thus offering added advantages and superior value to your customers. These additives, while not needed, can improve toughness or even encourage the finished product's longevity.

Stearic Acid

We rarely hear the term "acid" without feeling "caustic" immediately, but stearic acid is not the case here. Stearic acid is produced by using hot water and distillation to saponify the triglycerides in the fats and oils. Stearic acid may be produced either from vegetable or animal fats.

Combined with paraffin waxes, stearic acid may interact with wax to create a stable crystalline structure at the accurate temperature and appropriate ratio. It allows a strong candle that can survive cracking or to cave in. It succeeds in releasing mold.

In general, stearic acid is used at a pace of around 2-5 teaspoons per pound of wax. Stearic acid also assists in the opacification of transparent paper. For situations when you're over-dipping a candle to shield hidden items (shells, plants, seeds, etc.), you'll want to stop utilizing stearic acid because you can't see through the exterior coating.

Stearic acid is also used in the manufacture of candles to make candles tougher to resist slumping; for this purpose, it is widely found in votives and pillars. This is often used to render more visible opaque wax, improve burn time, and preserve fragrance.

Vybar

It is a polymerized olefin and is used in candlemaking to absorb stearic acid. Vybar can improve a candle's strength without leading to brittleness, which has the same consistency as stearic to offer improved opacity and scent retention.

Microcrystalline

A category of extremely refined waxes that are typically used to improve wax adhesion to wax or render waxes more versatile and elastic, or makes waxes stronger and more robust. Choose the microcrystalline waxes wisely. Before you use them, recognize what they are doing. When used correctly, they will make the candles better.

UV Stabilizer

UV stabilizers are used to avoid the deterioration of color by candles when subjected to sunshine (UV rays) or illumination, such as fluorescent lights. Whereas a UV stabilizer won't eliminate color fade, it will greatly mitigate it. These compounds are often labeled regulators of UV Protectants, UV Absorbents, and UV Inhibitors.

Synthetic Polymers

Some silicone additives may be used to deter color fading, to help loosen molds, to improve a candle's luster, to improve a candle's melting point, to produce mottling effects, etc. To obtain the best results, you would need to follow the instructions of the manufacturer for usage.

Colorants

Candle dyes come in many forms; the most common are liquid candle dye, pigments, and color blocks. Be cautious when coloring your candles; ensuring you use a colorant that has been certified for candles is important.

CHAPTER 11

MOVING INTO CANDLE PRODUCTION

The Candles And Recipes

How to Make Candles in Easy Steps

Candles that are infinitely customizable, classically elegant, and no sweat to create, they are for a cause the choice of a crafter. Here you will learn how to create series of candles at home afterward, the simple way.

1. How to Make Soy candle

Materials list: Soy candle

- One package of candle-making soy wax
- One pair of chopsticks or pencils
- One package of large candle wicks
- One spatula
- One thermometer
- One heat-proof container
- One bottle of fragrance oil
- One double boiler

Instruction

Step 1: Measure the wax

Make sure you have a clear, smooth surface to operate on until you start the candle-making process. You may also take a newspaper or paper towels to cover the region. Move what you don't want to use to wax over.

Measure how much wax the jar will like to cover, and double that Which is how much wax you're going to need to melt.

Step 2: Melt the wax.

Now, using the double boiler, pour the wax into it and permit to melt, constantly stirring for 10 to 15 minutes.

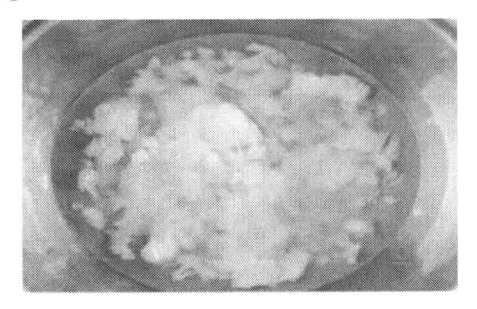

Step 3: Add fragrance oils

When the candle wax is melted, the time has come to add oils for the scent. Follow the procedures regarding how much to add from your wax kit. Only pour it onto your melted wax and mix for a couple of seconds. Although this process is optional, we will suggest it for a lovely floral fragrance.

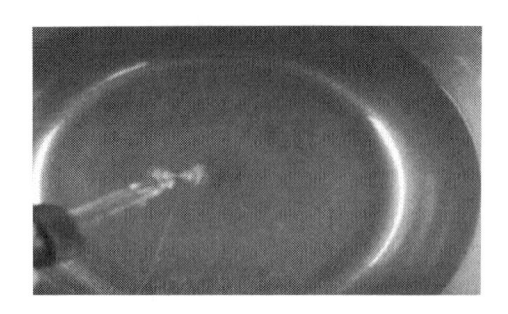

Step 4: Attach the wick.

Before you mix in the wax, the wick has to be secured to the bottom of the tub. You should tie the wick to the bottom of the bottle by dipping it in the melted wax and immediately holding it down. Let the wax settle in to harden for five minutes. Instead, you may apply a superglue.

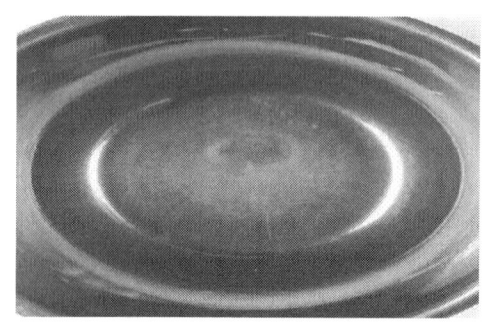

Step 5: Pour the wax.

Allow it to cool for some minutes before pouring the wax into your glass. If the temperature reaches 140 degrees on the thermometer, it is time to pour. Then, add the wax gently into the container. Hold the wick; just don't pull it around. To top off your candle afterward, leave a tiny amount of wax in the boiler.

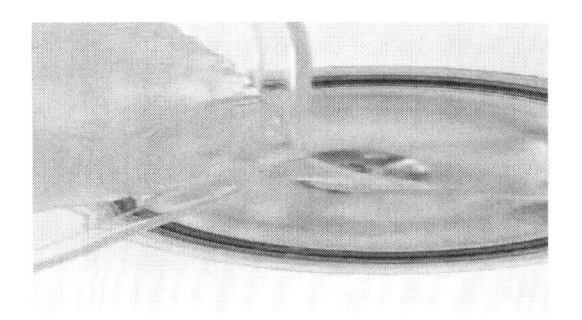

Step 6: Secure the wick.

You ought to lock it to keep your wick from swaying in the melty oil. Set out two chopsticks over the container rim. Put the wick between it, leaving it fixed as the wax solidifies. Enable the wax to set to room temperature of 4 hours.

Step 7: Add more wax

you can reheat and add your extra wax if your candle solidifies with a deformed top (think cracks or holes). It lets it solidifies.

Step 8: Cut the wick.

The wick on your candle will be less than half an inch in height. When the candle flicks or has a large flame when lit, then trim the wick.

2. How to Make Beautiful Ice candle

This informative feature shows how to place wax round smashed ice in a paper to produce a lovely ice candle.

Materials List

Candle Dye
Wicking
Pillar Wax
Candle Mold(s)
Thermometer
UV Stabilizer (Optional)
Fragrance Oil
Metal Spoon or Stir Stick
Pouring Pot
Wick Bars (Optional)*
Caution Labels
Crushed Ice
Butcher Paper or Newspaper
Sauce Pan
Paper Towels
Mold Putty* or Poster Putty
Cookie Sheet or Pan
Metal Cookie Cutter or Trivet
Utility Knife
Wick Trimmers, Scissors, or Nail Clippers

Instruction

Step 1 - Measuring out the wax.

You will start by weighing out the amount of wax you need to make the candle.

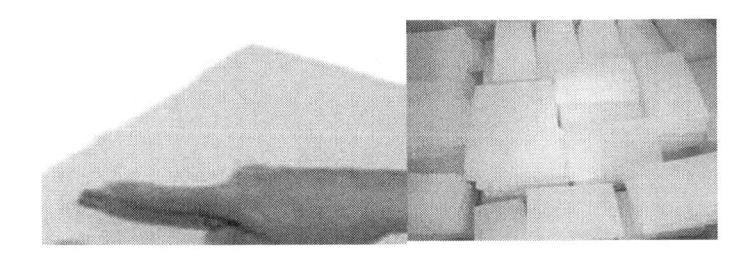

Step 2 - Cut the pillar wax

Cutting the waxes of the pillars can be difficult. For this instance, a utility knife is used to mark the wax. The formed piece is then put on the remaining slab, and pressure is exerted to help split the score through the wax. You can need to do so a couple of times to get the wax in sufficiently tiny parts to suit in the pouring bowl. You should measure the wax in the pouring pot, and you don't have to move it from another container.

Step 3 - Melt the wax

Based on the wax you have picked, the wax would need to be heated to 175 degrees to 185degrees. Put around one inch of water in the saucepan to make a double boiler, then position the pouring pot in the water. It is a smart idea to add an inexpensive metal trivet or cookie cutter to lift it under the pouring pot. Doing this means that the wax experiences no overt heat from either hand. Switch the heat to a temperature medium to low. The water has to boil, but it doesn't have to rush to a full boil. It will splatter out of the pan when the water is at a full boil. Frequently monitor the wax temperature to ensure it's not becoming too hot. Switch temperature to fit specific needs. You may start with the next steps as the wax is melting; just ensure the wax is never left unsupervised.

Step 4 - Prepare your mold(s)

When using a wick plate, ensure that the pin is straight and put it into the mold. Don't fail to insert a mold cap or putty into the bottom of the wick mold, so the wax doesn't leak out. When using a mold without a wick pin, thread the wick through the mold, ensure it is secured with a wick bar at the top and putty at the bottom. Ensure you seal the putty around the wick hole to create a strong seal. Position the mold on an old baking sheet or saucepan to hold the wax in case of leakage.

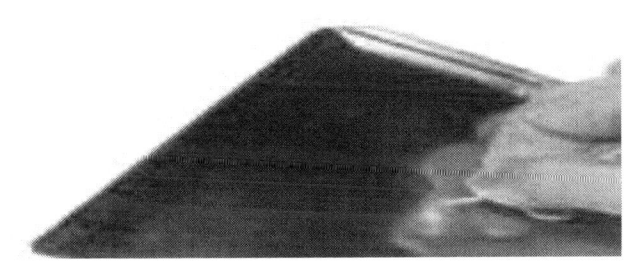

Step 5 - Fill the mold with ice

Fill the mold up. The perfect size for the bits of ice is around 3-inch to 4-inch pieces. As the wax melts, the ice will make gaps in the candle, and the pieces will not be too big.

Step 6 - Measure & add fragrance oil

When the wax hits the appropriate temperature, you are eligible to add the oil for the fragrance. You may apply 0.5-1.0 ounces of scent per pound of wax, based on the way you want to use. Putting in 1 ounce of fragrance in a pound of wax is most popular. The scent is more reliably measured by weight, although if the scale you use does not really measure a tiny volume, you may always use a table-spoon to measure it. A table-spoon is around 0.5 ounces. Pour the perfume into the wax and mix for 2 minutes to 3 minutes, or until the wax "absorbs" the fragrance entirely.

Step 7 - Measure & add dye

Subsequent, apply the sum of dye you want. If dye blocks are used, the block can easily melt into wax when broken into tiny parts. Mix the mixture until it is fully mixed, after adding the required amount of the dye. If you are using the color dyes, go to step 9.

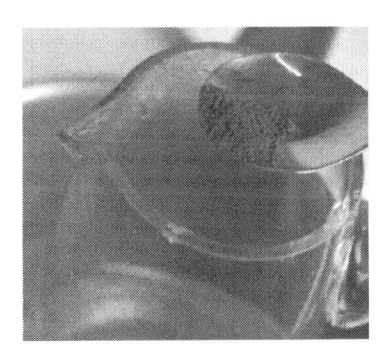

Step 8 - Measure & add dye

When using liquid dyes, simply add the number of drops needed. Because once it has been applied, you cannot extract the dye again. It should be used sparingly, particularly if you are hoping to get a light color. If it isn't dark enough, you can still put a little more. Stir the mixture until it is fully mixed, after adding the required amount.

Step 9 - Test your color

Most often, as you glance at the liquid wax, it will appear even darker than after it has cooled. You should drop a tiny amount of wax onto a sheet of paper or paper towel to check the color. Ensure the hot wax doesn't spill on your hands. Leave it to harden, and you'll see a more-clear color representation. If needed, you may then apply more dye.

Step 10 - Add UV Stabilizer

You may add a UV stabilizer at this stage if you like. When the candles are subjected to UV radiation or fluorescent lights, the application of UV stabilizers can help protect the color from fading. You'd apply about 1/2 teaspoon of wax per pound. You should continue to stir the UV stabilizer through the wax until it is absorbed/melted fully.

Step 11 - Pour the wax mixture

Pour the wax into the mold cautiously. While pouring, you should move the pouring pot steadily, so you don't repeatedly pour at the same spot.

Step 12 - Let the wax cool completely

Due to the ice, the wax is set quickly. Once the wax is completely formed, drain out the water gradually from the mold. While pouring the water into a sink, ensure to pick up any little bits of wax that may fall out with the water.

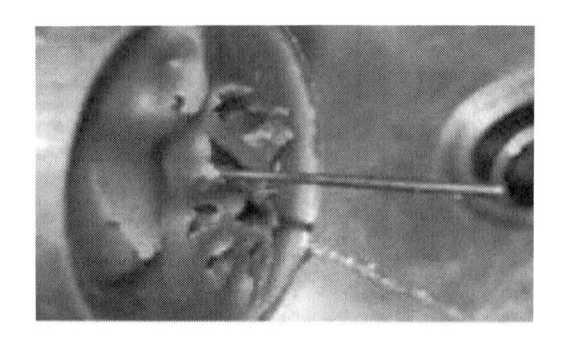

Step 13 - Options!

Upon reaching this point, you have an option. If you might rather leave the holes, then you have finished it. If you're using a wick pin, you may extract the candle from the mold, put the wick, trim the wick and add the precautionary sticker. Keep the candle in the mold if you want to perform a second pour to fill the holes further.

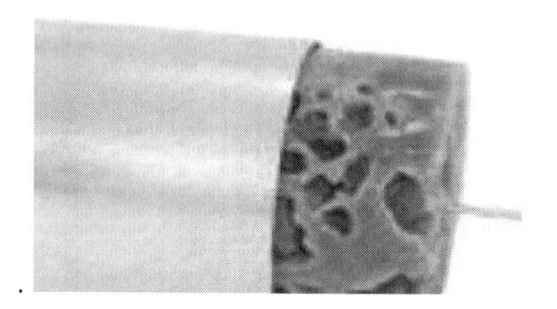

Step 14 - Second Pour

In the second pour, dye the jelly and add the Fragrance again. Pour the wax in gradually to ensure that the pouring pot is moved about, and don't pour continuously at the same spot.

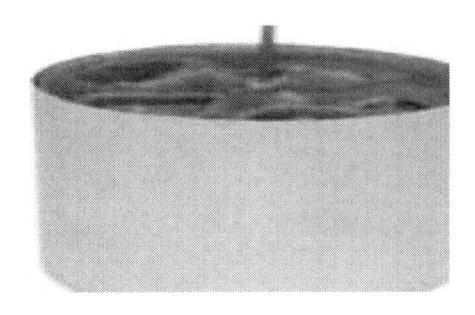

Step 15 - Let the wax cool completely

You can use wick trimmer, nail clipper or scissor to trim the wick to 1/4" in length. Just ensure you don't cut them too low, or they'd not burn well. You may then bring the lid back on top of the bottle.

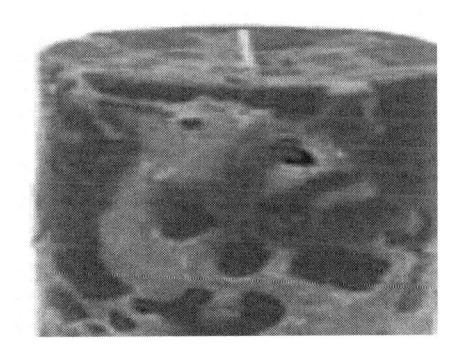

3.How to Make another Ice Candles

This candle is another simple to produce, and each candle should look beautiful and special. This is well adapted to certain candle types, but we have seen the most impressive results from the aluminum molds.

Procedures

Step 1

Prepare the mold as though it was a regular pillar mold that you pour. Using the wick pin whenever appropriate, as it will provide the candle another outlet to expel the water.

Step 2

The mold is filled with ice. The amount of ice differs according to the result that you want to obtain. The more ice you apply, the more cavities there would be so that the candle will become crisp.

Step 3

Add color, scent, and wax together and mix. Any mixture of color/smell should work for this project. Pour the wax (a 141-pillar wax, with better results) into the mold. Pour at various temperatures, with specific results. Pouring from 175 to 180 degrees can produce a lovely finish in most situations.

Step 4

Take away and hold the candle upside down by using the pillar ring, then allow the water to flow out. Seek to get as much water as you possibly out.

Step 5

Remove the candle, then attach the wick. Based on how many ices you've applied; how many cavities will occur?

Extra Suggestions

Once you have taken out the candle, put it upside down in the mold, and pour a specific wax color to cover the cavities. Putting the candle upside down would work better because all of the cavities on top of the candle are forming.

Place two or three rods around 1/4 "thick in the candle at various angles or produce a similar appearance. When the candle hardens, strain out the water and remove the rods and add the wax through the candle's holes.

4.How to Make Shot Glass Candles
PRECAUTIONS:

- Tie a toothpick to the wick. The toothpick around the shot glass the wick should stay in the center as you sit back. Trim the wick all but 1/4 inch (6.35 mm) down before lighting it up.
- More massive shot glasses make the candles safer.

- If you must recycle candles, recycle them into the same candle form, i.e., pillars into pillars, recycle tapers into tapers, bottle candles into container candles.
- Wax crayons are pretty excellent for dyeing candles, but if you use too much, they will prevent them from burning.
- Don't worry about having to break the glass. The bulk of shot glasses are constructed from borosilicate and are thus heat resistant.
- Use various types of glasses that use specific dyes or shades. Using some green wax to shape an olive tree, then bring a toothpick through it as it melts. Attach this to the Martini glass wax and let it settle inside the glass along with the wax.

Materials List:
- Wax
- Wick
- A small drop of fast-dry glue
- A shot glass or any thick glass
- Pan
- Wax dye in various colors
- An old measuring jugs

Instruction

1. Put all the old candles, half-burned, into a measuring cup.

Could use discolored wax if you intend to apply a wax coloring to it.

2. Put the measuring cup in a saucepan with hot water until the wax melts.

3. Wait to see where the wax nearly melts down fully.

You'll be able to apply the wax coloring at this stage (if the initial wax is discolored).

4. Place the shot glasses within the wicks.

Verify that you do have a clear shot glass or some other dense glass. Place a little drop of adhesive on the tip and force it into the middle of the glass to ensure that the wick remains in contact.

5. When the wax melts, spill the wax over each shot glass.

Be vigilant not to get the entire wick submerged.

6. When the wax is nearly set, push the wick into the middle of the bottle, then leave it to set completely.

Wax contracts when it cools, and after the candle has set, you may have to add more wax.

7. The finished stage

5. Making Borax Candle Wicks

Most conventional candle wicks are Borax-treated.

Materials list:
- Water
- Candle wax
- Kettle
- Borax
- Table salt
- Tweezers
- Cotton twine
- Double boiler
- Aluminum foil
- Clothespin or clip

Instruction

1. Heat out the water. Use a medium saucepan or tea kettle to heat 1 cup of water (250 ml) Have the water to not to a full boil but a simmer.

2. Dissolve the salt and Borax.

Pour the hot water into a tub of glass. Apply 1 tbsp (15 ml) of salt and 3 tbsp (45 ml) of Borax. Stir it up to dissolve.

This Borax solution would be used for treating base wick material. Borax curing wicks will render the candles burn brighter and for a longer time.

It will also reduce the volume of ash and smoke generated by the burning phase. Hold Borax away from kids and livestock, because it can have a harmful effect if swallowed or inhaled.

3. Soak the twine in the solution.

Take a piece of twine from the strong cotton butcher and immerse it in the Borax solution. Let the cord soak for 24 hours.

Ensure the twine length is greater than the bottle height you want to use with your candle. If you don't realize how big the candle is going to be, you should soak up to 30.5 cm of twine and trim it later.

Butcher's twine is a perfect base rope for candle wicks, but it will fit well enough with about every thick cotton string. You can use cotton embroidery, broken pieces of cotton fabric, or a clean shoelace which removes the plastic cap.

Soaking up the twine for 24 hours can produce the maximum results. After 20 minutes, you should theoretically cut the twine, but the effects won't be as ideal.

4. Dry the twine.

Use tweezers to remove the cord from Borax water. Hang up the cord and let it dry for 2 to 3 days.

- Before you proceed, the twine has to be thoroughly cleaned.

- To hang the treated cord in a warm, dry spot, use a clothespin or similar film. Put aluminum foil under the drying twine as it drips down to collect some excess solution.

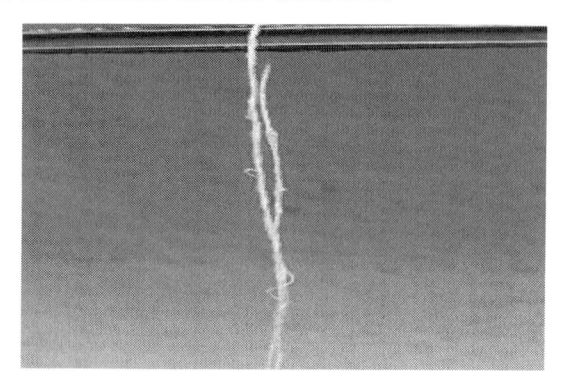

5. Melt the wax.

Break candle wax of 60 ml to 125 ml) aside. Melt the wax with the help of a double boiler.

- You could use a clean metal container and a small saucepan if you do not have a double boiler.

- Steam 1 to 2 inches (2.5 to 5 cm) of water over the stove in a saucepan, allowing it cool down and steam without boiling.

- Position the metal within the hot water bowl. Wait another minute before applying the wax to the pan to heat up.

- Melted wax will cause serious burns, so treat it with considerable caution throughout the remainder of the process.

6. Dip the treated twine.

The dry, Borax-treated twine should be gently dunked in the melted wax. Cover as many as possible of the twine.

You should use twine coated with Borax as it does without applying a wax coating. However, the wax allows the wick to be stiffer and more convenient to hold, which can even make it harder for the flame to ignite on the wick's edge.

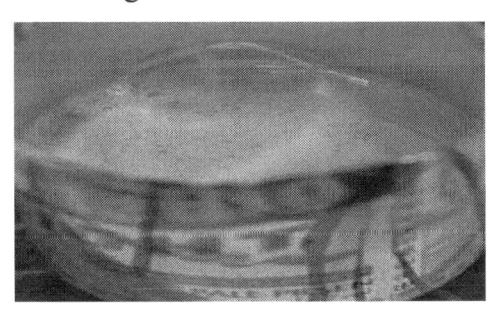

7. Dry the twine.

Hang the twine as before, and allow the wax to solidify long enough to dry. This would take only a few minutes.

Much as before, put a sheet of aluminum foil under the hanging twine to trap any extra wax that drips off.

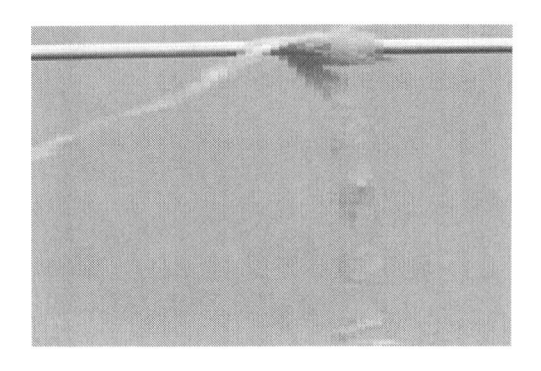

8. Repeat.

Plunge and dry the twine once or twice as often to create a thick wax coating.

- The cord will preferably feel stiff while maintaining some versatility.

- If you do not have enough wax to dip the cord again, you may put the cord on an aluminum foil sheet and sprinkle the remaining wax carefully over it. Allow the wick dry on the foil instead of making it hanged again.

9. Use the wick as needed.

When the full-coated twine is dried, it is primed and done to put into a candle.

6.Scented Tea Lights

The tea lights are simple to produce and are good as homemade gifts. Here are directions on how to create them together with gift box decorating ideas Producing end lights of good quality is far simpler than you'd imagine. What you need is to grab the correct components, then melt and pour the products into the cups. That's pretty much what there's to it, frankly. If you're making your own, you're going to be reluctant to spend the insane prices in stores that they're selling for.

Materials list:
- 12 Tea Light Wicks
- 15ml/0.5oz Essential oil or Fragrance oil (optional)
- 185g/6.5oz Soy Wax
- 12 Tea Light Cups
- Adhesive

Equipment
- Kitchen scale (optional)
- Digital kitchen thermometer
- Candle-

Gift Wrapping
- 2 Gift boxes (sized L6 x W4x D1.5")
- Wine Red Raffia ribbon
- Shredded kraft paper
- Red berries on wire
- Evergreen cuttings

Instruction

Candle Cups and Wicks

The first step is to mount the wicks and candle tassels. If soy wax tea lights start burning, any time you use it, all the candle wax will melt. If during this process, the wick is unintentionally shifted, it may eventually rest somewhere in the cup or tip over.

What you need to do is fix the metal wick-tab down to the cup bottom. You should place them on hot glue or use a Blu-tak type adhesive like this. Line the tea-light cups up on a paper sheet until you're done so you don't get the work area dirty.

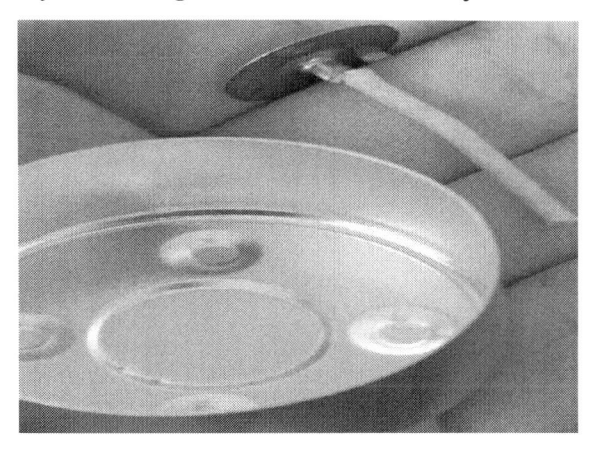

7.Melt the Wax

Soya wax should emerge in flat white flakes, so you'll have to weigh the quantity by measuring it on a meter or balling it up some. I still use a portable kitchen scale, but that's the essence of my business — it's 100 percent important when you're producing homemade beauty items. Tea lighting maybe a little more unreliable.

Put the wax flakes in the pouring pitcher and heat them in the microwave oven. DO NOT switch the microwave on and leave it unattended for many minutes. Between each burst, switch it on for 30 seconds at a time and mix the wax. It'll melt relatively soon.

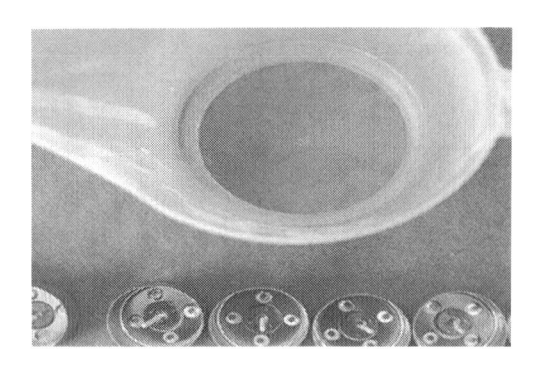

Adding the Fragrance and Pouring

Take it out of the microwave when the wax is fully melted, then place it on the work surface. You will also have to use your optical cooking thermometer to hold a temperature watch. If you add in your fragrance and put in too hot wax, your tea lights won't finish smoothly.

Allow until the wax crosses 120°F, until adding the oil into the wax. Stir for thirty seconds and retake the temperature. If it is around 100 °F, add the scented wax into the cups.

Cooling and Lighting

Candles must be allowed to cool for twenty-four hours before they are to be used. At this point, trim the wicks to around 2/16" and clean some wax with a paper towel that splatters off. Put them in a gift package, and decorate it to your taste.

8. Dipped Candles

Dipping possibly is the world's oldest way of producing candles. There's some suggestion the ancient Romans made candles that had been dipped. And, aside from the newer method of already mentioned container candles, dipping is probably the simplest and fastest way to produce candles.

9. Natural Soy Wax Tea Lights
Tea Lights are fun and straightforward to make

Essential lights of oil tea help build a bug-free bubble around your enjoyable outdoors. They're simple to create & this tutorial shows you the natural way to do it.

Tea lights are much easier to create than most people know. What complicates candle making is finding the best wax, wick, and oils. Using a decent product, and you'll be saved time and help prevent headaches. There is lots of fun here thinking for the first time that the candles would come out perfect.

You'll learn how to mix soy wax with essential oils in this recipe to produce all-natural lighting. When you pick the correct oils, you can also be able to keep your gatherings outside away from pests and mosquitoes.

Tea lights vs. Candles

Then why lights tea? You may create candles on a broad scale, but the tea lights are more realistic for outdoors. They're lightweight enough to bring in a bag or picnic basket, and they still have 4-5 hours of burn time each. Also, if you use them at home, the tea lights can look wonderfully scattered around your picnic table and outside the field. If you want to create bigger candles. All you need to add in is more soy wax and bigger containers.

Your Materials

Materials list:
- 12 Tea Light Wicks
- 185g/6.5oz Soy Wax
- Adhesive
- 15ml/0.5oz Essential oil, you can use a blend of Citronella or Lavender oil pure Citronella
- 12 Tea Light Cups

Equipments
- Metal or silicone spoon for stirring
- Digital kitchen thermometer
- Pipette
- Kitchen scale

When you use the regular tea light cup size, this recipe should give you around 12 light tea candles. This method helps you to create 16 of them.

Instruction

Step 1: Prepare the Tea Light Cups

Use a Blu-tak adhesive, or just a tiny strip of double-sided tape, insert each pre-tabbed wick into the middle of a light teacup. I consider using pre-tabbed wicks, but for some of my industrial candles, I use untreated wicks. This requires some time to have them trimmed and tabbed, which you can prevent by getting them pre-tabbed.

Place the cups either inside a mini muffin tray or on a sheet of baking paper. The muffin tray allows, and is convenient, to prevent them from running about.

Step 2: Melt the Soy Wax

Use a Blu-tak adhesive, or just a tiny strip of double-sided tape, insert each pre-tabbed wick into the middle of a light teacup. I consider using pre-tabbed wicks, but for some of my industrial candles, I use untreated wicks. This requires some time to have them trimmed and tabbed, which you can prevent by getting them pre-tabbed.

Place the cups either inside a mini muffin tray or on a sheet of baking paper. The muffin tray allows, and is convenient, to prevent them from running about.

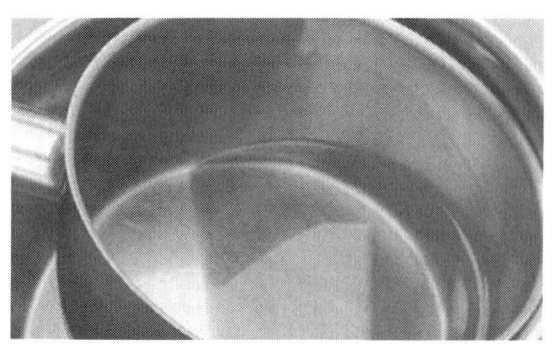

Step 3: Add the Essential Oil

You need to use about 8-10 percent essential oil for soy wax candles to get a 'Soft Cast.' Getting a throw is also a nice way to suggest they smell while burning. If you use in your recipe less than 8-10 percent of the volume of soy wax, the candles do not smell. They would not be as effective in deterring insects if they don't smell.

If that is 120 ° F (49 ° C), you apply the essential oil to your paper. Pour it into the wax and mix well for about 30 seconds before retaking the temperature. You want this to cool down to about 38 ° C.

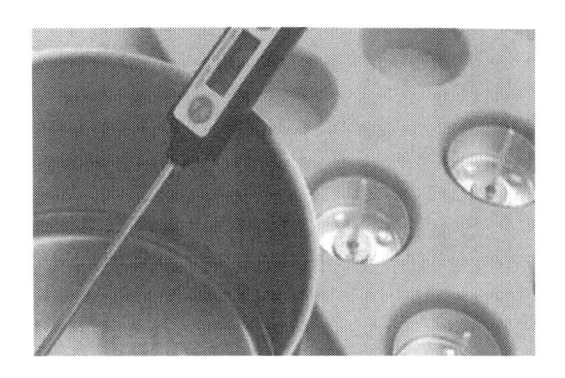

Step 4: Pour the Wax

Once the wax and essential oil have cooled, dump light cups gently into the tea. You should stop just before the top but go as hard as you can to fill up each. When after you poured the wax, the wick drops, softly move it out until it's straight in the middle.

Step 5: Cool & Trim

Let the tea lights cool down for at least one hour before going. The wick is then shaved down to 1/4" or even less. Instantly you will continue using the candles.

It's a typical issue with soy wax if you find any frosting going on the tops of your teapot. If you have one, you might re-touch it with a heat tool, but in all fairness, it is not a huge deal unless you want to sell it.

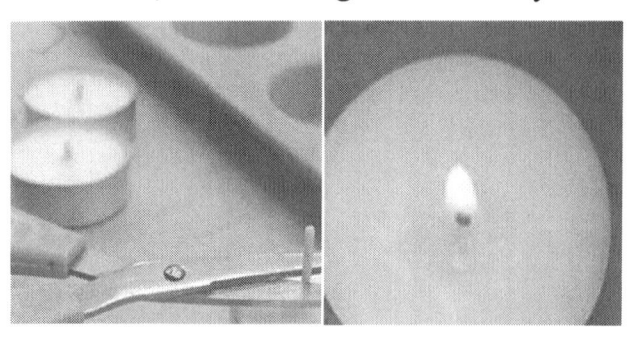

Clean up

Soy wax is relatively simple to clean. First of all, your pan: Clean off the excess oil with a paper towel or toilet paper while it is still dry. Then, wash it occasionally.

If one of your tea lights spills when burning, encourage it to harden until you attempt to clean it up. Often it comes up correctly, and even if it doesn't, then it's fluffy even easy to peel off. Hot soapy water from certain surfaces should scrub it out.

10. Make a Gel Candle

Gel wax is not wax, but a type of mineral oil. Working in certain respects is simpler than conventional waxes, which allows for more illumination than regular candles to show.

The clear gel will cause several exciting looks to be accomplished, from floating beads to underwater scenes.

Materials list:

- Wick
- Clear glass container
- Glass measuring cup or pouring pot
- thermometer
- Gel wax either mineral oil or resin if making your own.
- Embeds, gel dye, and scent

CAUTION

- Trim gel wick to one-quarter of an inch before the fire. This is quite fast! Hold it brief to prevent fires at the water.
- Never burn unattended candles.
- Don't use flame retardants! To avoid clouding and leaks, the raw products would be sprayed.

Instruction

Step 1. Melting the Wax

Run the heat. To do the perfect temperature, there are two methods to steam up the gel wax: a pouring pot on the burner, or a measuring cup in the oven. Both of these methods require caution.

Break the gel into substantial pieces and put it in the jar on a small to medium flame if you want to use a pouring bowl. Let the gel wax melt until a dense, syrupy consistency takes place. Don't allow the gel wax to get hotter than 230 F (110 C) using the thermometer.

If using the microwave, preheat to 225 F (107 C). Cut or chip off the required quantity of gel wax as the oven warms up. Place the gel wax in the glass jar when the oven is hot, then place it carefully in the oven. Let the gel wax melt for an hour in your oven. Using the thermometer to test the temperature of the gel wax regularly to ensure the gel wax is at the right heat point.

Hold an eye on your oil. Don't let it reach 230 ° F (110 ° C) temperatures, because it will burn and turn black, not to mention toxic.

Step 2. Secure your wick.
Do so while the wax melts. And if you don't need a button, it will make sure things don't go wrong.

Place a little dab of hot glue in your container. Take and put a single tabbed wick on the spot, keeping it for 15-20 seconds. It means just as you intend things to be. If you don't have a button, tie your wick's top around a pencil and put it on top of your container to openly hang it, and secure it.

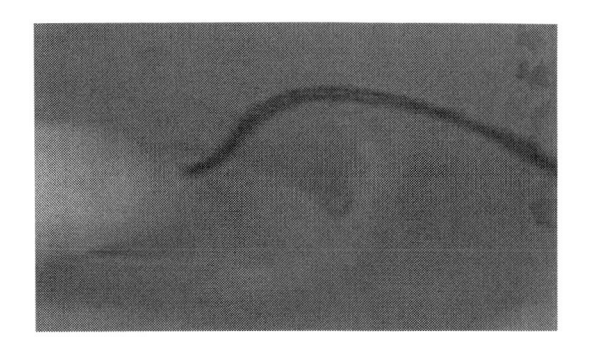

Step 3. Consider adding color or fragrance while melting.

You have several various paint and pacing choices, which can all result in different looks. If you want a standard feel, apply fragrance while heating and paint now.

- Use a scent that is consistent with hydrocarbons and not polar. Check 1 component scent with three parts of mineral oil after you have produced the gel jelly.

  If it blends well, then that's all right. If you purchased your gel wax from a shop, split it a little bit and check the dye until the sample could be ruined.

- Now applying the color would create a monotonous flame. The light must spread uniformly over all of the surfaces.

- Adding the color to the container would produce a swirling effect when just pouring in.

- When the gel is fully cooled, applying the color will build a ring around the rim.

- You may also apply layer by layer of paint, either in the pan (pour a little, add color, pour a ton, add color), or in the container. With each layer, the tone becomes more vibrant.

CHAPTER 12

CANDLE MAKING AS A BUSINESS

Candle Base Decorating Ideas

Pillars, balls, and other pre-made candles may be wrapped in molten paraffin or beeswax and then covered in decorative coatings such as Lavender buds, Oatmeal, Coffee beans, Lemongrass, Blue poppy seeds, Candle powder, Calendula petals, Hibiscus petals, etc.

Sculpted bases decorate blend 2 grams of beeswax with 3 oz of petroleum jelly and paint. For sculpting purposes, the wax should be pliable.

Paint the foundation with beeswax paint consisting of 4 pieces, 1 part oil, and candle dye. Enable the color to stay in and evaporate the oil for a few days. Overdip white wax on your lit lamp.

Pour dyed wax into mats, then use cookie cutters to cut shapes for decorating simple bases.

Cover with a whipped wax on the rim, and incorporate decorations if needed. Whipped wax may be made with 1 pound of the mixture. Melted beeswax with 1 tsp of oil and some coloring and beating till semi-cool. Place a spatula across the foundation.

You should dip the leaves and petals in transparent wax or cutout paper and add to the base surface. To cover the stick-on, over dump the finished flame.

You can make beautiful candles by getting a foundation overshadowed. Place base slightly larger than the foundation in a container. Fill the room around the candle with seeds, eggs, nuts, etc. and then add a 10% microcrystalline mixture of high melting point wax. Do not use stearic acid, because it would make the wax opaque. When it shrinks down as it cools, finish off with more paper.

The Most Creative Candle Designs Ever

Candle production is a long way off, and there are a lot of awesome designs out there to choose from.

Thanks to the lightbulb, candles may not be the most practical way to light up the home, but they are irreplaceable for building a warm or romantic environment.

How to Make Hand Candles

The problem with the balloon candle is it has no wick; you place a tealight within the wax case. You should spill the wax inside with wires flowing around the fingertips, instead of dipping the glove in wax.

You should apply enough red wax and make it appear like the fingers are weeping and render the hand candle more ghoulish for Halloween.

Here are steps in learning how to make your hand candle.

Step 1: Materials and Tools
- Candle wax
- Powder-free disposable gloves/exam gloves
- Candle wicks
- Pot for melting wax
- 20 gauge wire
- Clamps
- Duct tape

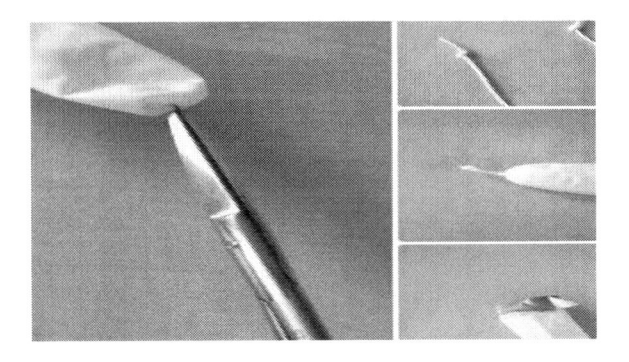

Step 2: Preparing Glove

- Punch a tiny hole in the tip of each finger; you want to have a candlewick.
- Tie knots in the wicks from the end about 1 cm.
- Poke the wick from the inside through the hole
- Cover the fingertip with duct tape covering the wick and the hole to prevent the wax from seeping out.

Step 3: Making a Holder

You should use some wire to create a loop to make it simpler and smoother to keep the glove open when pouring hot wax inside it. You slide the rope through the gap and also used a few clamps to pin it tight.

To make sure the wick(s) stay in the middle of your hand, you'll tie them together and curl the loose end around a pencil to secure them.

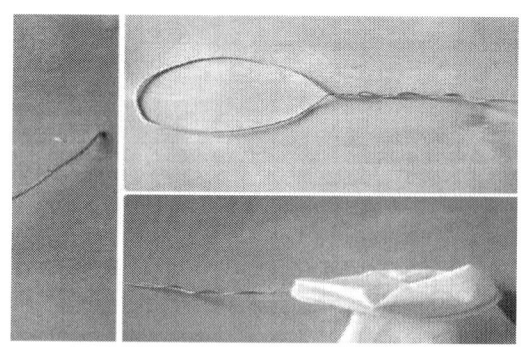

Step 4: Wax

A word of advice when pouring the hot wax, be vigilant because the gloves will break and spray the hot wax everywhere. Therefore, spill fingertips off yourself to stop burns.

The amount of wax you'll need depends on the thickness of the glove you use. To get the right number, you should fill a glove with water and then dump it into a measuring cup. Melting more than you like in case you leak out is an excellent concept. Put a plate or tray underneath your glove to trap some gout or spill.

Melt the wax in a jar on the table and spill it gently into the glove. Hang it up somewhere until it's filled to enable it to stabilize. It's growing a cork between the fingers and the thumb, as the thumb appeared to diminish.

Hand Gestures

You can stretch (and tape) your fingers until the wax sets if you choose to create hand motions, such as a symbol of love, peace, Vulcan salute, etc.

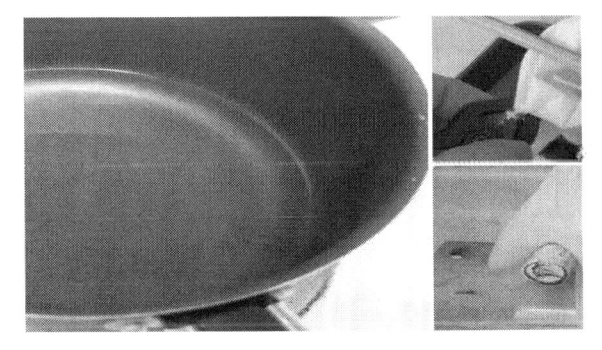

Step 5: Admire Your Handy Work

Once the wax has been thoroughly dried and hardened, the glove can be peeled/cut off. Trim the wick's edge off the edges. You should use a knife to cut it even if the bottom is rough so that it can balance without falling.

Melt a small volume of wax in color. Scoop up some of the red wax with a spoon and drizzle across the fingertips, allowing it trickle down the side.

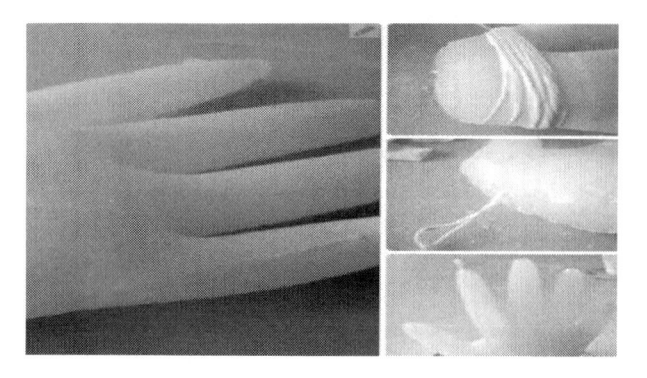

Step 6: Adding Red

Simply melt a small amount of red wax. With a spoon scoop up some of the red wax and drizzle around the fingers, letting it drip down the hand.

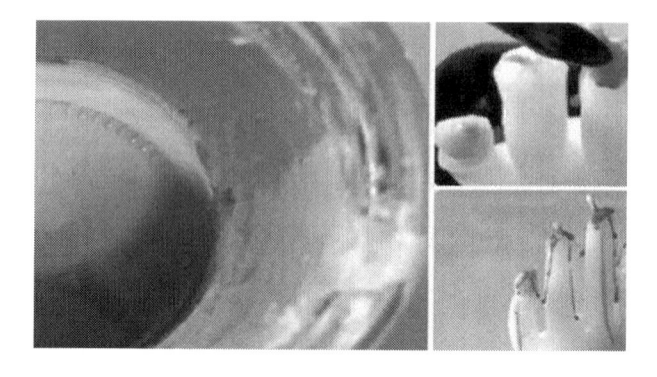

CHAPTER 13

CANDLE MAKING AS A PROFITABLE BUSINESS

This could be a bit biased, but a huge benefit of making candles compared to other hobbies is that you can effortlessly transform them into a part- or full-time enterprise. Most creative craftsmen enjoy business life's advantages. You can:

- Build and invest in something you own
- Be your boss
- Have the freedom to do work you enjoy
- Determine your schedule and day-to-day activities
- Spend more time with your family

Handmade products, including candles, are amongst the country's fastest rising small businesses. Candle revenues in the U.S. are valued at $4billion a year, according to the National Candle Organization. Here are a few more explanations why candles are a great business opportunity and high-demand market: People enjoy homemade premium goods and endorse locally run companies, that is why seventy percent of U.S use candle. And exclusively packaged candles are some of the most common pieces of home decor on the market.

Easy to start: You do not need a ton of machinery or resources to hit the ground running only required materials, software, and a workspace and it's fast and easy to learn the method. Simple to price, to market, and sell. You can sell your candles online via outlets like Etsy; via gift shops, art centers, and farmers' markets, or on your website store.

Planning For Candle Making Success In Eight Steps

You may have a profitable home business if you're involved in the artistic art of candle manufacturing. Candle market retail revenues in the US alone are estimated at over $4 billion, not counting candle products, according to the National Candle Group.

Candles with their useful and decorative features have become a must-have decoration in any home. They became famous as birthdays, Christmas, and housewarming presents.

Although candles may be manufactured at fairly low cost, manufacturing candles is a time-consuming method that can take some room. Some people buy already produced candles and install exterior cosmetic touches like brushed, dried flowers. Study the kinds of candles being made and create your line of candles.

Whatever the scale of the company, it is vital to develop a business strategy. This allows you to think about the future, set the groundwork for your business, and build a roadmap for success. We'll be outlining eight measures in this segment to create a great strategy.

Business strategy can sound overwhelming, but you should not fear. We recommend that it be held quickly and simply. Don't bother making any of the information right together.
Particularly in the early months, the priorities and business structure are likely to shift and evolve, so use this as a versatile blueprint to get going.

Step 1. Develop your "pitch."
Write a sentence explaining the essence of your company and the importance you offer to the clients. Think of it as the pitch of an elevator.

Step 2. Define your target market
The first step in developing your brand is to determine where your company falls into the broader marketplace for candles. Consider designing your line of candles in one of these three target markets:

Mass-market: Accessible candles usually contained in several retail stores. Such candles often use economical containers and packaging and carry typical fragrances such as pine and vanilla.

Mid-market: wide-ranging candles typically sold in retailers or even small gift shops and boutiques. You should find candles that have labeling of a better standard, special varieties of scents. And put a more excellent value on the story and identity of the business.

High-end: Clear indicators are luxury retailers targeting high rates or also upscale shops. High-end candles are usually prestige-level items that emphasize on the brand's packaging, scent, and tale.

To better determine which market to target, think of who is going to purchase your candles, how they are going to buy your candles, and how much they are prepared to pay. Then you'll have a clearer understanding of what materials to use and how to design the brand and packaging.

Beginning with a goal in mind is necessary but be able to change and adjust over time. Productive businesses continually adapt to best suit their business.

Step 3. Find your niche

You now know where your candles work in the marketplace, so it's time to recognize the specific "niche" of your brand, which makes your candles special and distinguish them from the competition. Here are some common ways we see candle-makers seeking the right niche:

- Special packaging
- Charitable support for a good cause
- Unique scent combinations
- Bright or whacky names for your candles

In the end, the aim must be to market candles that are so special and distinctive that buyers can't buy them somewhere else.

Step 4. Create a smart brand identity and name

Decide what to name your company and create a logo, color scheme, and corporate image until you've settled on something unforgettable and catchy, double-check whether a domain is accessible for a website (@.com URL is especially important) and run a quest for a brand. You don't need to file a trademark at once, but as your business grows, you'll want to have the option available.

Focus on what makes the company special while brainstorming titles, what you're excited about, and what resonates with the consumers. Don't get too descriptive with the identity. Concentrate on being intimate and truthful instead.

Step 5. Set a basic startup budget

We recommend that you build a budget for the first two months of business: estimate production prices, plant expenses, and overheads. Don't neglect to give yourself a monthly salary as a company owner and for your commitment and effort.

Step 6. Develop an initial product price and line

Holding your range of goods short and convenient is safest. Think of your friends and family in which candles are the most common, and whether they suit your target audience. You would also want to decide how much every item costs to produce and what a fair price is. Don't think about selling the candles depending on time and energy.

Step 7. Decide where to sell

It's not hard to search for places to market the candles. Three industries are here for you to consider:

- Your website
- gift shops, local craft shows, and farmers markets
- Online marketplaces

Try letting the network realize you're selling candles now, too. Your families, mates, and peers will have important reviews on your product line early on, which can be some of the most influential brand ambassadors.

Step 8. Incorporate, explore permits and licensure, and get insurance

Most of this depends on the position and the desires of particular businesses. For advice on the incorporation and liability policy, you can consult a solicitor, accountant, and policy specialist. You ought to discuss conditions for small enterprises to receive state and municipal approvals and licenses. You have several business arrangement choices for sole proprietorships, C corporations, limited liability companies, joint partnerships, and corporations.

The Candle Business Marketing Guide

Understand Your Customers wants

If you're selling scented candles, wedding dresses, or some other commodity, it's vital to your marketing success to know who it's you sell to. If talking about the buyer's character, there are three key things to keep in mind:

Demographics – This includes age, sex, geography, etc. These are relevant to learn because they can help establish effective ways of organizing promotions. Begin by developing a fictitious (or even real) consumer or "buyer identity" who is more likely to buy your candle and write it down.

Spending Behavior – Do your customers usually purchase high-quality candles? Are they doing deals? Are they shopping online? What other related items will they be buying? Knowing such habits would allow you to choose the best position with your marketing. Be sure all those specifics are used in building the buyer profile.

Attention –How do you invest your time with clients? What's taking your attention? These are some of the most significant recognizable things that will drive the marketing placements. You may create Facebook advertisements for your clients, for example, since you know they're wasting time on social networking platforms.

Know What Makes Your Candle Products Distinct

Your favorite! First, you get to think about the reasons why you began your candle company. As the specifics and price of your candles usually correspond with different target audiences, this relates quite strongly to your customer profile.

Write a list of all the "interest propositions" which characterize your candle products.

Know The Best Sales Seasons and Fragrances For The Candle Business

Enjoy the Busy Season

Getting a strong grasp on the schedule in this market will help you travel miles. For candle sales to skyrocket, there are lots of periods during the year, so it's crucial to know when to purchase a couple of extra pounds of wax.

Sell your Candles in the Slow Seasons

Do not let the slow months pin you back. Now is not the moment to slow the marketing strategies down. Focus on the products which sell throughout the year and promote them for a wide range of uses.

Here are few marketing ideas for the slow business season:
- Give your email-list a discount.
- Give a little birthday presents to buyers.
- Gift suggestions for instructors or students to move forward.

- Create enjoyable advertisements and use unusual holidays as a humorous excuse.
- Hold your social network sharing that holds everyone's favorite candle "top of mind" these days.

Promote Your Candle-Making Business Online

The most relevant marketing place in 2019 was online. This refers to physical and online stores, respectively. Noting the buyer's men, value offerings, and seasonal significance, here are some innovative ideas for selling candles for use in the digital age:

Four Steps to Make When Crafting Your Business's Voice on Social Media

Choose Your Social Media Channels – Candles are an enticing commodity seeking to pick from and make sure to select the right visual platforms. Images are a huge draw on sites such as Snapchat, Facebook & Twitter, and it's important to engage in these vital three.

Brainstorm Themes and Ideas. Bearing in mind your brand, come up with concepts that resonate with your community and have an emotional impact.

Make a Content Calendar. It is necessary to schedule your post ideas to keep your audience interested and active. You want to post enough, so they look forward to your posts, but they're not getting tired of you. Creating & keeping to a calendar can help you keep the duration stable.

Design and Write! Make sure you design your posts & compose your captions, then schedule the posting.

Getting New Candle Buyers With Internet advertising

Internet sites are booming on ad room sales, and there is enough to purchase for everybody! Sign on Google and Facebook for free ad-accounts. These platforms are the finest for gaining clicks directly from your website, as well as segmenting your audience and displaying ads specific to them. And because the cost is dependent on the number of clicks on your ad, it's just as expensive as it's profitable.

Ensure Repeat Customers With Email Marketing

Subscribing to newsletters is a huge favorite predictor for the brand. If it is automatic from sales or optional from the page, you'll accumulate the customers' email addresses. Get on with them! Begin a weekly newsletter; probably send out once a month. Send out the same one twice a month if they are good. Free tools such as Mailchimp allow sending and creating emails a breeze!

Explore Additional Initiatives to Marketing Your Candle Business

Blogs.

Blogs will be an excellent way to get people to learn from you! It's not often that we get a taste into where our money goes; send the customers that.

Forums.

Like blogs, forums could be a perfect way to connect with customers who know about the brand and the industry. The distinction here is that you can still notice several other company owners interested in their jobs in this area and exchange valuable insights and strategies.

Marketing Concepts For Brick and Mortar Candle Businesses

In addition to the aforementioned online strategies, here are a few campaign concepts that might help brick & mortar the candle making businesses.

Keep your Customers Interlocked With Your Candle Business

In an online space, consumer interaction can be simple. Commenting and sharing can take the day just seconds and will pull in hundreds of dollars. Engagement in-person needs a little more effort but a lot more enjoyable!

These are a few suggestions:
- Sell at markets & local events.

- You can invest in ads in your community and printed flyers.
- Host candle-making classes in your free time

Unique Marketing Techniques To Start Your Candle Business

1. Use stealth techniques to snatch your rival's customers.

Each business wants to snatch clients from their rivals, but most don't consider it their number one concern. If you have a rival that sells a comparable commodity but doesn't produce positive outcomes to their clients, you can target those customers.

2. Amaze and give your customers giveaways

Gifts are nothing new. They are seen by other companies to generate interest. So, then you push them to the next point what occurs.

This is giveaways brought to a higher point. It's just about knowing what the consumers want, and making free things thrill them! Some of the candles are set high to accommodate that. In the meantime, the business is not losing any money.

3. Bring in another brand

Want more brand awareness, or need to attract a different audience? Invest in another company (which isn't a competitor!) that will help you accomplish your objectives. Take for starters Spotify, and Starbucks. Through the convergence in technology, people who like a song they hear at Starbucks will use the brand's app to search and find out what it is all about and repeat it on Spotify, giving the brands more popularity.

4. Launch a referral program

If you want fast-growing followers, referral marketing might be your best option. The referral services help you to advertise your company to customers. It's an easy idea, but it's not often seen for small companies. The reality is, you don't require a big firm's expenditure to compensate for celebrities or sports figures. "True" influencers are even more powerful than A-listers.

How much money can I make selling homemade candle online?

Start selling candles you have made online.
Homemade candles are more in demand, internet sale is faster, and producing candles is cheaper. So, launching a candle company online from home makes perfect sense.

How you can sell candles online

This will be your eCommerce entry stage. Starting a company online is a perfect opportunity to make money from home or gain a passive profit. Hence, we can find out in this post how to launch an online company by selling candles. Based on your ambition, commitment, and ability, this time next year, you should be able to operate a famous handmade candle company!

Types of candles that you can sell online

Once you launch an online candle company, you need to make sure that the candles you produce are in high demand. Otherwise, people would not be purchasing the candles that you produce. The following are a few different types of candles which require very high online sales demands.

Type 1 – Scented or aromatherapy candles

People are using scented candles to add fun and pleasant aromas to their living spaces. For special events, they purchase scented candles. So, you may make candles with a broad variety of fragrances, including;

- Sandalwood
- Vanilla and nutmeg
- Lavender
- Tobacco
- Mahogany/Teakwood
- Mandarine
- Peach
- Coconut and lemon etc.

Both such candles may be purchased, make scents as oils from local supplies stores, or on Amazon. we will give you all the connections you need in a little bit.

Type 2 – Selling decorative candles

Consumers are purchasing candles literally to decorate their living spaces. So, you should also start producing decorative candles. While producing decorative candles for sale, you need to think more about the product's looks.

Decorative candles usually come with several different types, shades, and accessories. Use the festive candle images on Pinterest and Instagram; you will get fashion inspirations.

Type 3 – Soy and Vegan candles

Throughout the candle market, soy and vegan candles are in very strong demand. Unlike regular oil, paraffin, and beeswax candles, soy candles are produced out of wax derived or extracted from soybeans. Soy candles usually flame longer and cleaner too. Hence soy candles of the highest quality are typically priced at a higher price than standard candles.

Selling Homemade candle Online: Pros and Cons

The candle industry provides numerous candle sale opportunities, and each has both advantages and disadvantages. When you start and develop your company, the aim is to figure out growing one better suit your needs for time, capital accessible, growth potential, and ability set.

Pros

- The cost of building up the web site initially can be fairly small. You can take photos of yourself, set prices, and build whatever looks you may like to accomplish.

- You will schedule the hours you want. Since the website acknowledges the orders, you just need to produce your candles and send them on time.

- You should hold or keep the production or inventory of finished candles to a minimum, because you don't need to put all candles on the shelves to market, unlike a retailer.

- You may also configure your candles by taking orders from the Website. Because you don't need a store to offer the candles after you've got an order, you may produce the candle.

Be sure, though, that you have the ingredients on hand to produce your regular and personalized candles so that they can be delivered within the timeline specified on your blog.

Cons

- Establishing a website doesn't guarantee sales of any sort. Competition is high in this segment, so you have to find strategies to push traffic to your web. Ways of achieving so involve utilizing pay-per-click ads, digital marketing by following up on earlier purchases.

- Although the initial setup of the site may be fairly straightforward, bringing tourists to the web involves a continuous cost and one that must be tracked on an ongoing basis.

- Choosing the domain name is one significant thing that can not be taken lightly. Through search engines, that may be a component that helps buyers to locate you. Make sure to "brand" the line right from the outset, and you can begin to experience consumer loyalty when they love the candles.

Craft Shows, Festivals, Flea Markets

It is very crucial to do some research before selecting the shows you want to perform in to ensure a positive case. Small craft shows usually don't take much work, so going into the event is not that costly in general, and the chance is minimized. Typically speaking, the larger the series, the more costly it is to get into it, and the more work you will be conducting when you agree to join.

Getting any experience or link to the show is important when choosing which show to do. This may be just witnessing and experiencing the encounter. Check out how candle vendors are participating, speak to any of the departing vendors, and find that buyers appear to be gravitating to the price points. The more knowledge you have, the higher the odds you have of choosing the series you will have the most results in.

You need to tell your story

To share your handmade method and personal experience through images, on the blog of your store, and in marketing, using storytelling. Develop a solid, reliable social identity to advocate for you and your company. Customers in many situations purchase from smaller labels as they purchase into the culture behind the brand or choose to get a piece of you, the maker. Highlight what sets you apart from the rivals and rely on something larger brands can't do: make the interaction unique and one of a kind.

CHAPTER 14

CANDLE BUSINESS MARKETING ON SOCIAL MEDIA

Candle Making Business Promotion On Social Media

Several entrepreneurs see social networking ads as the next big trend, a strong yet fleeting fad that needs to be manipulated while it's in the spotlight.

For some, it is all a buzzword that has little realistic value, and with that, there is a complex, steep learning curve.

It indicates that social media marketing has tremendous potential for revenue success, but there is a lack of awareness among marketers as to how to produce such outcomes. Before we move into how you can effectively inject yourself into the social network marketing environment, let's discuss how social media marketing will help you and your company.

1. It increases products Recognition

This is of the tremendous importance of a chance a company owner has to syndicate their material and maximize their exposure to their future buyers and partners, also their existing ones. Social networking networks are only a different platform for the company to express its opinion and raise visibility to its product and service.

It is imperative for your company because it allows your company more open to potential clients and buyers; it also allows you more recognized and recognizable to others who have previously done business with you. For instance, regular Twitter users can hear about your business for the first time only after they come across it on their newsfeed. After seeing your appearance on several different networks, maybe an otherwise apathetic consumer would become more acquainted with your company and brand.

2. It Improves Product Loyalty

Brands that connect with their social networking platforms have higher customer loyalty scores. Companies can take advantage of the opportunities offered by the social network when it comes to communicating with an audience. A transparent and realistic approach for social networking appears to be successful in keeping customers loyal to a brand.

3. It Creates More Opportunities to Convert for more sales

Any post you placed on social networking networks is an incentive to attract a customer or company. In creating the following, you obtain exposure to potential clients, existing clients, and current customers at the same time. You may also communicate with them all simultaneously. Any picture, blog post, photo, or message you want to share is an invitation for others to respond to what you've shared, and any response will contribute to visitors to the sites, and ultimately conversions.

Not all social networking interactions with your company can result in a conversion, but every successful communication can improve the likelihood of future conversion. Even if the click-through rate is low, a game-changer is the sheer number of chances you have.

4. Higher Conversion Rates

In a few different forms, social media marketing can carry in a better conversion rate. The most important approach is by the dimension of humanization. When you connect on social networking sites, the name is more humanized. Social networking is a platform that companies may behave as customers do, and it is important because consumers want to do business with someone, not just a company.

5. Increased Inbound Traffic

If you do not have a social networking presence, the inbound traffic would be limited to users who are already familiarized with the business and individuals that are looking for keywords on search engines that are on your list.

Any social networking profile you have is another route that leads back to your site and every article you make, click, tweet, or connect, is another way for a potential user to engage with you. The more quality content you get on social networking sites, the more inbound visitors you'll receive, and the more visitors you'll get will mean more leads, which would inevitably contribute to more sales.

6. Better Customer Experiences

Social networking is a means of communication, including telephone calls and emails. Any user experience you have on social media is an opportunity to demonstrate your quality of customer support to the public, and it is an opportunity to strengthen your partnership with your consumers.

For instance, if anyone on Facebook wanted to complain regarding a product, you might answer the issue, openly apologize to them and take steps to remedy the problem. Or, if anyone praises you, you may like to ask them for any complimentary items and suggest them. It's the intimate connection that tells the customers that you truly care for them.

7. Better Customer Awareness

Social media helps the organization to obtain insightful knowledge on what prospective clients are involved in and how they handle themselves in a virtual setting. For instance, you may track comments to see what people specifically say about your company, or track for comments aimed at your industry.

You should break the content into the topic-based lists to see what types of content attract the most attention from consumers, and then generate more of that kind of content. You can calculate the sales you are getting based on the numerous promotions shared on different social media sites and find the right combination to generate revenue for your company.

If you are a brand, there are several benefits of being on social media, but all of those advantages boil down to one aspect – you get more publicity for your company, which turns into more profits. Your bottom line would be gratitude for investing a tiny bit of time and money into your work on social networking.

Why You Need The Social Media Marketing Plan
Social media marketing plans are in-depth drawings of all that you plan to achieve by doing your business on social networking activities. Without a clear approach, social media marketing sounds like a hopeless task, and the potential for success is suffering greatly without direction.

There are six steps to establish a social networking contact program, which we will address throughout the rest of this article. Notice, a social networking approach is just like every other component of a business plan, meaning you need the information to affect a business.

Step One: Make Aims for Your Social Media Impact

Much like every other communication strategy, establishing goals is the first move toward a successful one.

Specifying your targets allows you a straightforward way to calculate your marketing plan's performance, so it's a way to keep track of investment gain (rate of returns). Social networking marketing helps the company achieve several targets, so you may want to consider some of the more important ones:

- Potential customer engagement and increasing customer with the company
- Improving customer loyalty and increasing sales
- Increasing followers, which will increase the number of potential customers
- Increasing traffic to a website
- Promoting the customer service division
- Brand awareness increases

Facebook marketing

Facebook Marketing Techniques For Candle Making Business Sales

Facebook Marketing Tips for candle Businesses

What is Facebook marketing all about?

Facebook marketing applies to create – and actively utilizing – a Facebook account as a medium of communication to establish interaction with and recruit clients. For this reason, Facebook effectively provides users with the ability to build individual profiles or company pages for businesses, organizations, or any community that seeks to establish a fan base for a product, service, or brand.

Who Is To Employ Facebook For Candle Marketing

Any business should be using Facebook, with nearly a billion potential customers. It is at least as important as making a web page for businesses—and far simpler to create. If you're promoting a major company or a tiny corporation that hires only a couple of employees, you can guarantee some of your clients are still on Facebook. Usually, marketing via Facebook is:

Brands. Food, appliances, home products, restaurants—nearly any brand can be marketed via Facebook, transforming passive consumers into enthusiastic fans following news of sales and innovations and connecting with their mates.

- Local Firms. If a shop is family-owned, or a more prominent company's subsidiary, you may use a Facebook account to transform a loyal client base into a fan base that visits the store more frequently.

- Brands. Food, appliances, home products, restaurants—nearly any brand can be marketed via Facebook, transforming passive consumers into enthusiastic fans following news of sales and innovations and connecting with their mates.

- Local Enterprises. If a shop is family-run, or the affiliate of a more significant business, you may use a Facebook page to turn a dedicated customer base into a fan base that visits the store more often. Musicians, actors, writers, syndicated columnists—anyone who earns their income by being popular needs to be remembered by as many people on Facebook as possible.

- Non-profit organization. Charities, advocacy parties, and public awareness programs alike will leverage Facebook's existing networking capabilities.

How is a Facebook marketing campaign?

Facebook sites are also connected somewhere on the Internet to client web pages; thus, it is typically a smart practice to use any of the same material in all cases to preserve compatibility. A business website can be checked for as soon as it is up, so you can't invite friends into it, unlike a personal profile. Company pages don't get "mates," they get "fans," so there's a gap in the choice.

The marketing team leader should start by enjoying the business page on their profiles to build an initial seed for the fan base; all workers should be invited to join in. When a person likes a link, Facebook automatically adds this occurrence to their profile—and any one of their friends will see this action. The word just continues spreading.

Any Facebook user who likes a page can get to see some business material posts and be informed of updates via their news feed.

Communication Continuity is the most critical part of Facebook marketing. Creating a Facebook page and then leaving it alone does nothing for a company. A website will periodically publish new content in a range of various formats to attract followers so that more users can see and share the link. Posts will reveal exciting deals, showcase unique items or individuals, share fun information, include bonus codes on product and service offers, and everything else that captures fans' attention.

The news feed reveals posts from their friends / etc. to them. They communicate with several of them, although some are more recent. Therefore, a company's article is expected to only be available on the news feeds of their followers for only three hours after they publish it. It is likely to be used by slightly specific parts of their fan base, based on the time of day they publish.

Facebook is also valid because it is the number one most common site that companies want to start selling on. Facebook has an active audience of over one billion. That's a big market for your company, so it means you've got to be cautious of where you're investing your money ads, so you've got to have a good sense of your brand's demographic. Understanding who'll be involved in your Facebook product will phenomenally improve your revenue.

Guide to using Facebook for business

Setting up a Facebook Account costs nothing. You may also use it once you have built your Page to post material, link to your site, and interact with fans and followers for free because it makes a Facebook account an extremely useful resource for any marketer who has a small budget running.

You also need to build a Facebook Business Page before you can continue using Facebook's paid advertisement techniques, like Facebook advertising. Therefore, planning your Facebook Page is the first step to learning how to use Facebook for companies. Follow these steps:

1. Create a Facebook Business Page
- Go to facebook.com/pages/create. To get started, you need to sign in to a different Facebook account, but your login profile will not show on the online company page.

- Choose the form of your page: Business/mark or Community/public figure.
- Fill in details of your company.

2. Add brand images

Upload your cover and profile photos. Always ensure that Facebook uses the correct picture sizes, and they look their best.

3. Complete your Page details

Select Edit Page Info and fill in the section below:

- **Description**: 255 characters which are describing who you are and what you are doing.
- **Contact information**: fill in all the areas you want people (including your website) to contact you.
- **Extra options:** Attach your working hours, pricing range, and privacy policy if applicable to your company.

4. Create your Facebook username

Your username lets a user find you on Facebook. Select on Create @Username page to create one. This can reach up to 50 characters.

Facebook marketing ideas for the vanity URL you can use:

- Select a name for the search-friendly Page. It would be the brand name in most situations.
- Use a consistent username throughout social networks where appropriate.

5. Add a call-to-action button

A call-to-action button offers a fast and simple way for users to reach out to you, search for your goods, or otherwise engage in business. To set up one, click on Add a button under the cover picture.

6. Review your Facebook Page settings

Options in your Facebook profile give you personalized power of who knows what's on your account. Look about in detail to make sure you recognize the privacy and protection settings.

This is how you can quickly set up your Facebook company for your candle production. Your Facebook account is set up and ready to go.

Types of Facebook posts

Now that your Facebook page has been created, you need to worry about what kind of content to publish.

Here's a rundown of the diverse forms of content that you may use to communicate with your fans. A lot of new features has been added from time to time for marketing on facebook.

Facebook text post (status post)

It is the most common kind of posting on Facebook. It's only next: no images, no photos, not even a connection. A text-only post cannot guide users to your website or push sales, but it can be used on your Blog to ignite interaction. For better partnership, you would need your candle pictures posted.

Tips for Marketing on Facebook

As a business device, Facebook wins the popularity battle as a central factor for most corporate marketing strategies. However, due to the durability of Facebook messages, you may notice that you are struggling all the time to come up with new material and fresh ideas for your business or brand profile.

Timing

Although it relies on your target market, material, and priorities, you need to evaluate the timing of your updates carefully. Look at the target group, take note of their personalities, and the period the posts connect to them.

Good Images

You've most definitely seen this one a million times, but you can't stress sufficiently the value of adding photos to the posts you place on Facebook.

These are a few useful tips for images on Facebook.

1. Share images of real people/your candle products
2. Be succinct
3. Use lifestyle imagery rather than product imagery
4. Concentrate on people's faces
5. Use nostalgia to your advantage
6. Build galleries
7. Encourage a short reply

Good Contests

People want to get things for cheap. All find themselves to enjoy and connect with a sponsored Facebook account that they wouldn't have been aware of until they had the chance to win anything.

The key reasons users on Facebook's' heart' products are that they can get a deal, coupon, or offer. While the principle of growing interaction is strong, through the use of Facebook competitions for companies, there are seven real returns on investments shown.

Give Them Uncommon and Valuable Content

This might sound somewhat trivial, but the amount of businesses and products which focus on old or outdated knowledge indicates how many lost opportunities are there on Facebook.

Promote New Product Announcements

Facebook boost posts tend to be helpful, particularly for smaller businesses. While most experts would warn against utilizing the app, small businesses will profit greatly from boost posts announcing new items.

Running Facebook Promotions and Contests

Businesses with Facebook accounts today have several more choices, so by uploading a video or text so inviting people to like or vote on that post, they can run a contest easily. Through running the competitions, you will get even more attention on your website.

While Facebook terms and conditions have to be respected, and from time to time varies.

Twitter Marketing

Twitter Tips: Make Your Tweets get to the Top

Using Twitter for Business

Once it comes to Twitter marketing, it is vital to have your profile and audience. We'll look at how you can maximize the performance with Twitter by taking a few easy steps.

- Optimize Your Bio
- Follow Hashtags or Trends
- Get Your Colleagues Involved
- Tweet Regularly
- Track Mentions and Respond
- Retweet
- Ask for Twitter Love

Offer Special Deals and Discounts

Hold any Twitter contests, such as the next fifty people who retweet this article can get a 50% off coupon or make them post pictures of themselves using the product or in the shop and get a random draw.

Use Images and Videos

Using the videos and pictures to get visual. We receive three or four times more Facebook impressions than email messages.

Photos and videos have proven to earn more likes, impressions, and shares than a tweeter of plain text. Although a group manager may do a decent job engaging fans, a post about enjoying the weekend is much less successful than in-stream content where anyone may see a film trailer and find out where the film is played in their neighborhood.

Choose What You Share

You should upload a lot of material and not just text messages on Facebook. The network can accept several various media types that can be inserted in messages, such as text, candle images, or pictures.

Promote Content

You will push a lot of traffic to your site store when you leverage Twitter well.

Building an Audience

Creating and retaining the audience can sound time-consuming only for those who are familiar with marketing, whether from scratch or another existing audience. It's not enough to post many times a day to promote growth.

Instagram marketing

Why Instagram Is Not Just for Aspiring Photographers

Instagram is a wonderful device to use, but you must be able to use it. Many businesses want to support people who share photos for them, so you can upload your own for your company easily and gain even more followers.

Use Instagram to increase customer sales and interaction.
- Expose Something New
- Balance Fun Images with Images from Your Business
- Inspire Your Potential Customers
- Debut Videos
- Use Hashtags Related to Your Industry or Niche
- Create an Amazing Profile
- Build a Following
- Create a Flexible Posting Plan
- Use Filtered and Non-filtered Images
- Market Your Brand with Trends
- Follow Followers Back

- Expose Yourself to Other Brands
- Embed Instagram Videos into Blogs or Websites

Much of the marketing material is the same as Facebook, Twitter, etc.

LinkedIn Marketing
LinkedIn Tips: Network Like Clockwork

LinkedIn is not solely for career hunters and practitioners. Certainly, millions of professionals use LinkedIn to develop their networks and careers every day, but do you know you can use LinkedIn to develop your company, too? LinkedIn provides a vital contribution to the digital marketing campaign, from making contacts to gathering leads, forming relationships, and building a more magnificent brand image.

LinkedIn is a social network for professionals. It's all about job growth, personal relations, market conversations, and business-related events of many kinds. It's not like other social networking marketing outlets like Facebook, Twitter, or Instagram; there, marketers have easy exposure to users who they can appeal easily to through status changes, photos, as well as other casual posts.

1. Keep refining your LinkedIn profile

First impressions are important, and this is an excellent chance to improve your profile.

Keeping up to date on your profile is one of the most impactful ways to boost your contact performance. Your viewer is engaging with it, not just your name. People are doing business with others, and profiles matter.

- Aim for approximately 100 percent completeness and refine the profile continuously.
- Add new abilities, achievements, and details of your most successful job.
- Bring the personality in. Authenticity counts only as much as knowledge.

Make sure your page contains the following seven items filled out:

- Logo
- Company description
- Website URL (link to your website)
- Company size
- Industry
- Company type
- Location

To complete your profile, go to LinkedIn's Company page and pick "Overview":

2. Find highly targeted customers and connections

In the field of digital ads, targeting on LinkedIn is unprecedented. Small companies will purchase a product or service at zero based on the actual market, company type, and work position [of the people] they know will usually buy.

3. Create an active LinkedIn page

That is the profile on LinkedIn for your organization.

Your page will provide potential consumers with enough opportunity to know more about your company and the people who work there, and to connect with related material.

4. Define your audience and goals

- Raising awareness or generating leads; targeting is vital.
- You decide what you intend to do; the target is more readily identified. If your company offers a social media optimization device, the target could be to increase brand recognition among LinkedIn participants with job titles such as "social media boss" or "social media lead."
- Audiences lead to better lead generation.

5. Post-high-quality content

Effective content should be strongly targeted, and it can achieve two objectives. Firstly, it will show us how to approach an issue properly or how to do their work. So instead, it places you in the space as a leader of thinking. If you give them real value, each factor inevitably leads to more sales.

6. Add a LinkedIn "Follow" button or social media buttons to your website

Another perfect way to cross-promote your LinkedIn Company Page is to make it convenient for your followers to swap material at some stage during the reading or viewing process.

By attaching the "Join" LinkedIn icon to your home pages, or by utilizing sticky social network networking buttons in your blog articles, you set yourself up for long-term growth and scope.

Youtube Marketing

YouTube Tips: Video Made the Marketing Star

YouTube is essential to companies, especially to marketing teams. And you have no choice but to search for more exposure for your YouTube posts.

- **Make Compelling Titles.** No matter how good your video looks, it's useless if no one clicks on it. So, you must optimize your video titles to bring in viewers.
- Here are some helpful tips for building ideal YouTube titles for greater accessibility:
- **Find the right keywords:** In the description, keywords show crawlers what the video is all about. And right keywords also tell your viewers what to expect, so that's a win/win.
- **Keep the title short.** The desired duration of the video titles would be no more than 60 characters. Readers should have a glance at the full title.
- **Create clear and descriptive titles.** Don't force viewers to make up for it. Let's let readers know about the video.
- Tell readers why they should watch this video. They need a justification to waste time looking at the stuff. They want to learn if that's going to help them.

Using the rule to get a successful title:
- Identify a key concept for your video
- Look for short and concise keyword phrases which address this topic

- Choose a title which answers the most crucial question for viewers

2. Create Perfect YouTube Thumbnails

Active thumbnails make it easy for users to right-click and create your YouTube page. Thumbnails should be important to the quality of the video and its description.

Include short descriptions and related images of your thumbnails to help people understand what your video is about.

Take people's eye, and say a tale using your thumbnails. You have to let them ask what's next.

Ideally, the title and thumbnail together would tell a complimentary tale.

Here are some useful tips/measures for custom thumbnails:

- Make use of standard video dimensions/sizes - either 1280 x 720 or 1920 x 1080. Smaller sizes might look blurry and useless.
- Make use of high-quality images (HD) only.
- Add the video title to your thumbnail or image because it tends to draw further viewers.
- Photo/image formats should include JPG, PNG, GIF, BMP, and TIF.
- Using the aspect ratio 16:9 makes it works better for YouTube players.

- Keep your look consistent, and adhere to all your thumbnails
- Use emotion. Include new faces and focus on the eyes.

3. Limit Videos to be within 5 Minutes

If you want to have the best out of your videos, focus on their overall screen period. Based on report, most YouTube videos have a length of about 5 minutes

If you just repeat yourself by making long images, it won't help. People need fair and reasonable reasons to be interested in your film. With video duration, you can try to find out what works best for optimum interaction.

Here are a few tips you should follow:
- Build high-quality content with any single video
- Optimize your videos to be less and not more than 5 minutes
- Make them informative, interesting and short

4. Brand Your YouTube Channel

The next thing you can do is to mark your YouTube channel and make it beautifully appealing and inspire viewers and take you seriously. It helps increase the visibility of the company and invest more time with the viewers.

Use your company logo for your channel. When you're a professional photo writer, instead of a tag, you should use a headshot.

Only add names and explanations to the videos to help viewers locate you. You should also have ties to your website and social network alongside the banner picture.

You may also use self-branded overlays when communicating about a specific product in your video. Most viewers don't think about this, but as they see the videos, they give you an incentive to attract customers.

Apart from creating and developing visual branding, having an insight and informative and meaningful bio of your business or your personality is important. Let people see what attracts you, and let them motivate you. Fast and entertaining.

5. Include Calls-to-Action (CTAs)

Adding calls to action to your videos helps you create greater trust and gets you more engagement on YouTube. These can be annoying sometimes, so strive to avoid them properly.

No matter what targets you have, be transparent and succinct about the main steps people need to take to get more followers or more subscriptions.

In the video, or at the end, you should attach your website link (URL) or invite subscribers to your channel to help people understand the next move.

When your target is to draw more subscribers, consider doing it smartly. Your long term contributions will be respected.

6. Share Videos via Social Media

When you want to expand your platform, posting your videos on social media is important. As a savvy marketer, not only posting the new videos on social media but also becoming involved in social networks and groups is important.

Every media network has its community, so you need to find out which one is better for you and whether it can value your efforts.

Use the following helpful tips to improve and promote your videos:

- Attach YouTube videos to presentations on SlideShare
- Share your videos on Twitter and Pinterest
- Link back to your original YouTube video and make mini promo videos on your Facebook page
- Promote and share your videos on relevant Facebook, Google+, LinkedIn groups, and communities
- Integrate your videos into your blog content
- Publish your videos on Scoop.it
- Add your YouTube channel to your Instagram bio
- Add your videos in other people's posts on associated websites

Use websites like Amazon, Etsy, and several others.

Pros

- The startup costs which are associated with any of these are generally minimal, with nothing upfront in many cases.
- These sites are heavily visited.
- They set up systems for the credit card and payment methods.
- A platform such as Etsy is great because all the products have to be crafted.

Cons

Like for all internet shopping, there's stiff rivalry for candlemakers. The trick is to consider something that's special that you have. It would be important to find a way to differentiate yourself through any sort of differentiation, such as providing exclusive jars or facilities, or by exploring certain avenues to start attracting buyers and like your stuff.

How to market & promote your candle making business

Your key move is to find out which market you want to draw. Is the average consumer a tactical shopper for cost-savings mainly, or is she more involved in the sensory experience? If the clients are the former, they should speak about good pricing. If the above, you can show your product line perfectly and ensure sure the usage of colors and fragrances is pleasing.

Try building up a site on online auction sites such as eBay, Amazon, and Etsy. In these places, you can encounter a lot of rivalries so hold the costs as small as possible.

How to keep customers coming back

Your goal is not only to attract clients but to make them repeat clients. Since candles are disposable products that need to be regularly replaced, the current consumer relationships may be profitable over time. So make sure you're meeting their wishes, loving the price of the items they get from you, and remembering how to reach you when stocks run low.

That's why any order must have simple contact details, whether it's your website, email address, or telephone number (or all three). With this knowledge, you might attach a business card or sticker as part of the packaging. Make sure shoppers and lookers alike get your business card while approaching clients of individuals, such as at art shows or flea market experiences. And seek to get their names and approval to connect them to an email list as subscribers you might be sent out before peak candle-buying periods such as year-end holidays or Mother's Day.

CONCLUSION

Getting innovative is a gift, and it is a very nice way to love a hobby only by taking the time. The best thing about creating candles and soap is that it's an enjoyable hobby to do at home and the pleasure of getting the artistic side put to work and seeing a finished product you've made. When you start producing your goods and see the results, you will be glad and happy with yourself. It can start as a hobby, but it can easily turn into a profitable business.

Candle and soap production is already a great activity to do, which is right up there with the creation of side candles. When you start making candle and soap, the possible hood is that your buddies and coworkers would love you for it and ask all questions about how they can get engaged and maybe pay you for any of the stuff you've made. Still, it is more than possible that they are only going to demand your candles and soap products.

The most significant benefit of producing soap and candles at home is that it's an inexpensive way to make your quality products, using solely specific ingredients you prefer to use in your kitchen or on your skin.

Soap and candle making is important in certain ways of one another. The production of a candle and soap has a decent number of parallels where you can finally know that both making soap and creating candles are enjoyable and simple to do. Given the fact that one of the two would be your passion, you can also transform them into a business where you can provide additional cash and savings for your wallet.

While producing soap and candles, it is crucial for you to realize that you can add your innovation here. A touch of your taste is crucial to come up with a performance that will deeply satisfy you. The soap/candle producing methods are certainly simple to know and appreciate. In spite of the reality that producing candles and soap is almost the same, it would be much simpler for you to learn how to create a candle and soap because you already have the experience of how to create it.

Made in the USA
Middletown, DE
20 July 2020